THE OLD HOUSE BOOK OF

CLASSIC COUNTRY HOUSES

THE OLD HOUSE BOOK OF

CLASSIC COUNTRY HOUSES

Plans for Traditional American Dwellings

Compiled by Lawrence Grow

THE MAIN STREET PRESS
Pittstown, New Jersey

First edition 1988

Published by
The Main Street Press, Inc.
William Case House
Pittstown, NJ 08867

Published simultaneously in Canada by
McGraw-Hill Ryerson Ltd.
330 Progress Avenue
Scarborough, ONT M1P 2Z5

Printed in the United States of America

10 9 8 7 6 5 4 3 2 1

Library of Congress Cataloging-in-Publication Data

The Old house book of classic country houses: plans for traditional
  American dwellings / [compiled by] Lawrence Grow.
      p.   cm.
    Bibliography: p.
    ISBN 1-555-62054-X (pbk.) : $8.95
      1. Architecture, Domestic—United States—Designs and plans.
    2. Architecture, Colonial—United States—Designs and plans.
    I. Grow, Lawrence.
    NA707.044 1988
    728.3'7'0973—dc19   88-15497
                                                                            CIP

Contents

Introduction

As America moves into the twenty-first century, a nostalgic spirit is taking hold. As in the decades preceding the last turn of the century, this mood is evidenced in popular architecture. During the 1880s and '90s architects and builders reinterpreted the predominant style of a century earlier—the Colonial. And, once again in the 1980s, there is a resurgence of interest in the Colonial style, particularly in its more formal and neoclassical elements. Round-headed window sashes are becoming as common in homes today as skylights were in the 1960s. Entrances are regaining pilasters and fanlights; many exterior walls are trimmed with elaborate cornice moldings and window casings.

Some architectural observers term the return to Colonial forms "postmodernism" or "neoclassicism." The new style, by whatever name, is certainly no more a faithful copy of traditional Colonial architecture than was the Colonial Revival of the 1890s. There is little substance to the body of work which is now being turned out along Colonial lines. The average Palladian window installed today, for example, has neither the profile nor trim of its 200-year-old Georgian Colonial prototype. This is not to say that modern work is not legitimate, simply that most of it is not Colonial in a formal sense. But you must know what is authentic to understand what is derivative.

Classic Country Houses presents twenty-six examples of American Colonial architecture, dwellings built from the 1720s to the 1850s. The buildings which are more formal and elegant than others are properly termed Georgian Colonial and were built from the early 1700s until late in the century. Others are markedly neoclassical in decoration and are called Federal. Most of these date from the 1780s to the 1840s. A third type of house displays Roman or Greek forms in such elements as columns, moldings, and pediments and correctly can be called an example of Roman Classical

Revival or Greek Revival architecture. Like Federal houses, these buildings usually date from the late 1700s to the mid-1800s.

All of the houses included in this book are characterized by a symmetrical composition, a balance created by windows flanking each side of an entrance. The same formal parallelism is usually found in the interior. Most of the houses are two rooms deep and have four rooms on the first floor divided by a center stair hall. The second floor, usually devoted to bedrooms, repeats the first-floor plan.

This type of house may have walls of stone, brick, or wood. The roof is usually a simple gable roof with chimneys positioned at each end. Houses of the Greek Revival or Roman Classical style, however, sometimes have a pediment roof, and eighteenth-century Georgian Colonial houses may have a gambrel or a hip roof. Chimneys are sometimes centered on the roof rather than placed at each end. When the chimney is centered, the house is likely to have a front stair and entrance hall which does not extend to the back.

Interior decoration differs from house to house, of course. In stone houses, windows can be very deeply set in plastered or wood-paneled reveals. Even in frame or brick houses where walls are thinner, window casings may be quite complex and deep in profile. Interior shutters that fold back at each side of double-hung sashes are often found.

The number of lights or panes in a window sash will vary since windows are among the most commonly replaced building elements over the years. Nonetheless, it would be rare to find original Colonial window sashes with fewer than four lights. More commonly, the number is six over six or nine over six lights on the first floor and a similar number on the second floor.

Baseboards and shoe moldings generally can be found in every room of a Colonial house, and chair railings are also common.

In principal rooms such as the parlor, master bedroom, or dining room, the dado or lower part of the wall may be paneled or wainscoted. Raised paneling is the most common form of woodwork for walls and doors. Room ends paneled from floor to ceiling are also found in the parlors and bedrooms of many early Colonial houses. The room end is often made up of such components as a closet, cupboard, and a door to a set of closet stairs. A paneled room end is almost always found on an outer wall.

Cornice moldings, ceiling medallions, and extra features such as arches, niches, and transoms are found in a majority of the houses illustrated in this book. They are sophisticated elements, however, which are not found in the average Colonial house. And contrary to popular belief today, ceilings were usually plastered so as not to leave beams exposed. The "rustic look" was not considered attractive. Flooring in Colonial houses is most often of pine laid in a random-width fashion. A hardwood such as oak was sometimes selected for principal first-floor rooms, especially in larger, more formal houses. Brick and stone were reserved primarily for entry halls.

Fireplaces are found in most principal rooms and in some bedrooms of the Colonial dwelling built before the early 1800s. The largest fireplace with an expansive hearth for cooking is located in the kitchen. The kitchen fireplace wall often also contains an opening for a warming or bake oven. By the 1820s, use of the fireplace was beginning to wane. The wood-burning Franklin stove had come into use by this time and it was easily vented through a chimney stack. Central heating systems were not installed in most houses until the late 1800s.

Although none of the houses shown in the following pages was originally equipped with indoor plumbing, bathrooms have since been added to some. Sometimes it was relatively easy to tuck a bath into what was originally a walk-in closet or pantry;

in other cases a bath was provided when a wing was added to the original house.

Among the most appealing features of many of these houses is the stair hall and its staircase. The center-hall floor plan lends itself to use of a generously proportioned flight of stairs. Homeowners had a number of styles from which to choose. In most of the houses, the stairs ascend in one straight sweep, but in some dwellings, the staircase takes a particularly graceful spiral form or ascends in two stages with a landing between the floors.

All of the houses illustrated in *Classic Country Houses* are from the archives of the Historic American Buildings Survey housed in the Prints and Photographs Division of the Library of Congress in Washington, D.C. Most of the drawings were executed in the 1930s and '40s. All the facade elevations and floor plans available for each house have been included in these pages along with some detail drawings. Readers who wish further information or illustrative material on a particular house are urged to consult the collection at the Library of Congress. References to the specific HABS survey numbers are included at the end of this book.

1. Berkeley Plantation

From general appearances, Berkeley, the ancestral home of the Harrison family in Charles City County, Virginia, is a model Georgian Colonial dwelling. A five-bay structure of brick, it is perfectly symmetrical, two rooms deep, basically square, and laid out according to a center-hall plan. Completed in 1726, it is certainly one of the earliest American Georgian Colonials. Many of the decorative features of Berkeley, however, date from a later period. The windows and doorways were enlarged in the early 1800s, and the brick accenting around the windows was also added at that time. The dormers, the main entrance and its surround, and the entry steps date from the early 1900s. These later additions, however, are very much in keeping with the original character of the house.

The brickwork is laid in Flemish bond with glazed headers, and presumably the brick was produced on the site. A belt or string course of brick divides the first floor from the second. Two brick chimneys serve five fireplaces.

The floor plans are somewhat unusual in that the first floor contains the dining room and the second floor the kitchen. More commonly, this order would have been reversed. The kitchen shown in the plan is probably of a later date; an earlier kitchen was probably located in the raised basement. No plan is presented for the attic floor; presumably this was an area devoted to storage and to the housing of servants.

Some of the interior features are evidence of the major remodeling which occurred in the early 1800s. Arched alcoves, simple neoclassical mantels, and pedimented or corniced doorways were added at this time in the Federal style.

Berkeley was built for Benjamin Harrison IV. Both Benjamin Harrison V, a signer of the Declaration of Independence, and William Henry Harrison, ninth president of the United States, were born here. The house was sold by the Harrison family in 1845 and is now a National Historic Landmark.

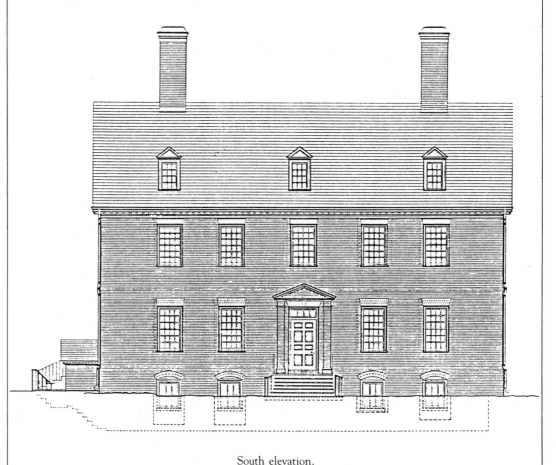

South elevation.

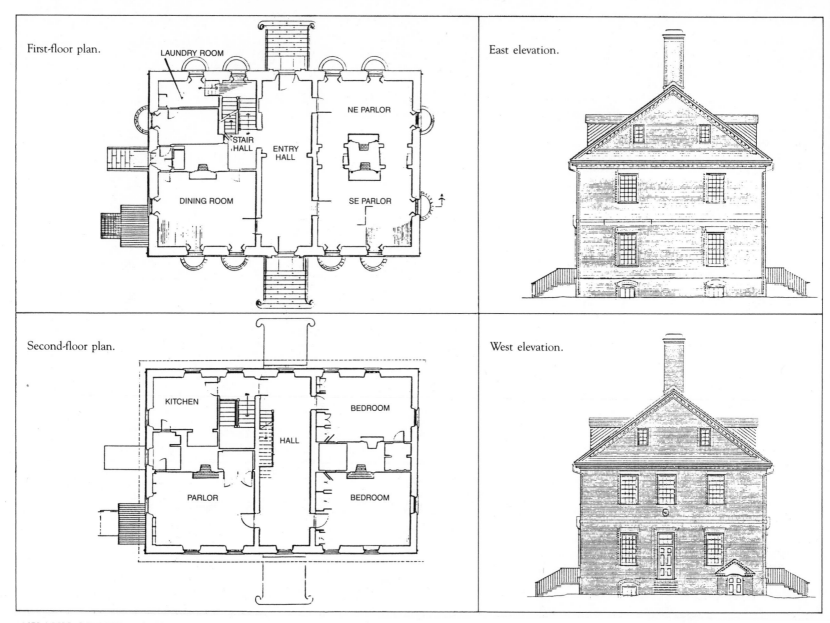

First-floor plan.

LAUNDRY ROOM

NE PARLOR

STAIR HALL

ENTRY HALL

SE PARLOR

DINING ROOM

East elevation.

Second-floor plan.

KITCHEN

BEDROOM

HALL

PARLOR

BEDROOM

West elevation.

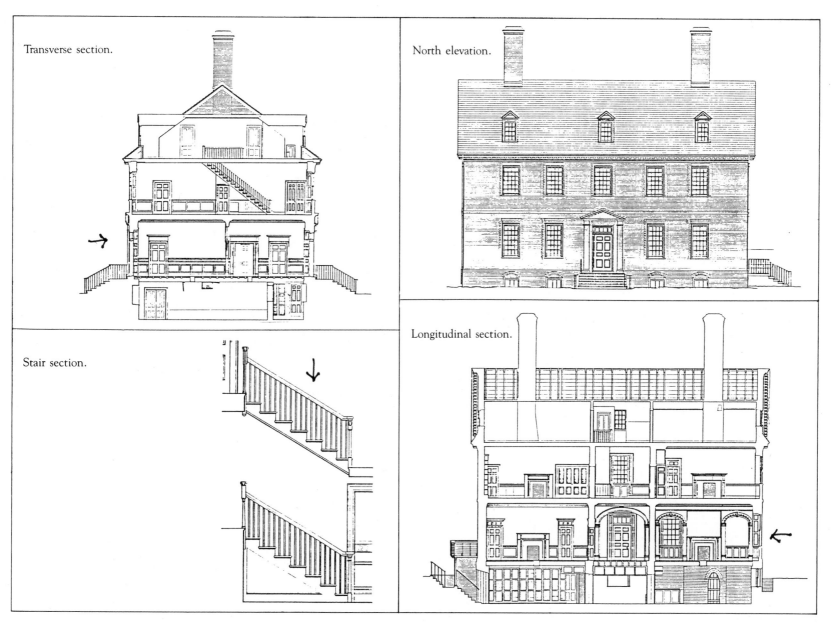

Transverse section.

North elevation.

Stair section.

Longitudinal section.

2. Fort Bowman (Harmony Hall)

Simple and rigorously symmetrical in design, Fort Bowman, located in the vicinity of Strasburg, Virginia, was built in the mid-1700s. It is not a building distinguished by family or architect, but is representative of a vernacular house type commonly found in the Mid-Atlantic and the border states. The front porch, a later addition in the Federal style, gives the building a sophisticated and graceful air that would otherwise be lacking.

Although by no means a mansion, Fort Bowman is also not a house of the average country dweller. The use of brick segmental arches over the basement and first-floor windows exhibits a finer architectural touch than was common in the eighteenth century. Like most other Georgian Colonial houses, Fort Bowman has a spacious center hall from which all rooms radiate.

The basement floor probably housed the kitchen, laundry, and storage rooms. Note that this floor is partially above ground level, a feature of many Georgian Colonials. The first floor may have included a large parlor with fireplace, a dining room with fireplace, and a bedroom. The second floor appears to have been divided into four bedrooms, one of which was supplied with a fireplace. This room was probably the master bedroom.

Southwest (front) elevation.

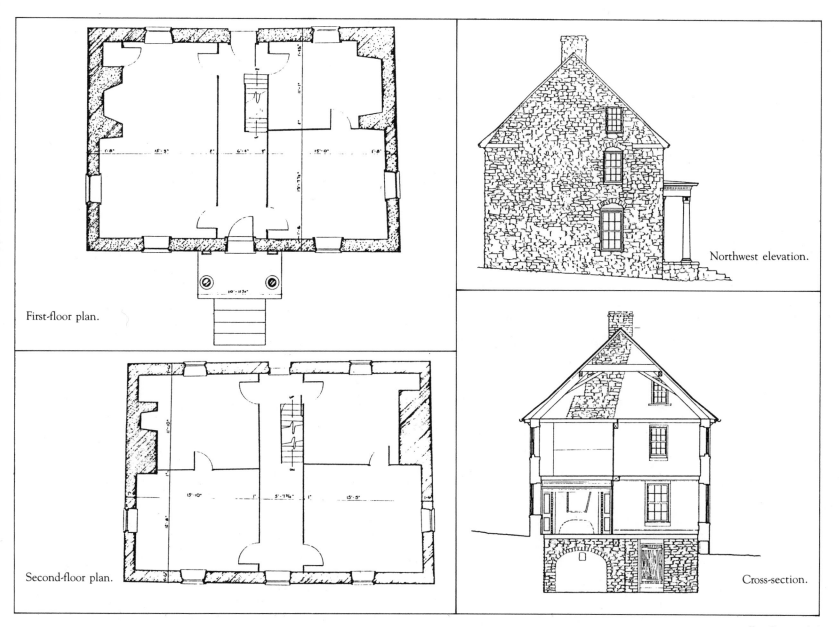

First-floor plan.

Second-floor plan.

Northwest elevation.

Cross-section.

3. Rocky Mills

Rocky Mills was built around 1750 near Ashland, Virginia. Torn down in 1928, it was then rebuilt near Richmond. The building is distinguished by its very fine Georgian Colonial design. How faithful the reconstruction was is difficult to determine, but the basic lines of the building are presumed to be true. Among the distinctive elements is the handsome Palladian window which is centered over an equally imposing main entrance. The windows, 12 over 12 on each floor, are generously proportioned, and each is defined by a stone lintel with keystone and a stone surround. The quoins, belt course, and watertable are also of stone. The main wall areas are of brick laid in Flemish bond.

As in most classic country houses of the Colonial period, the floor plans are simple, all the rooms opening up from either the front hall or a rear stair hall. Two massive chimneys serve the eight principal rooms. There also appears to have been a cooking fireplace in the room designated "No. 3" on the first floor. This may have been the kitchen. The room marked "No. 5" on the second floor was probably used for sewing as it is too small to have served as a bedroom.

Originally the house had similar front and rear entrances parallel to each other. Note, however, the disproportionate size of the rear entrance compared with the rear windows. The same disproportion is seen on the north side of the house. In both cases, the seeming discrepancy may have been a result of reconstruction.

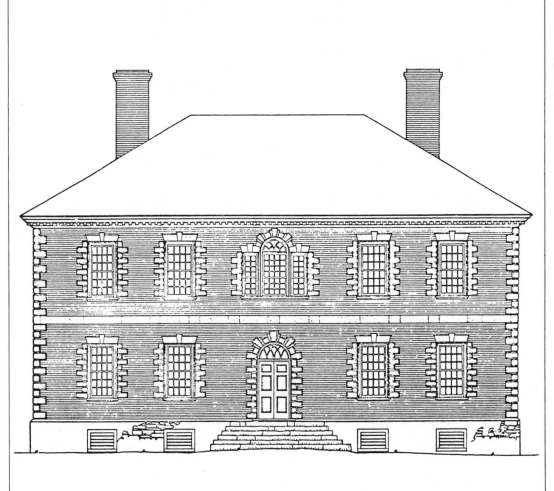

East (front) elevation.

Second-floor plan.

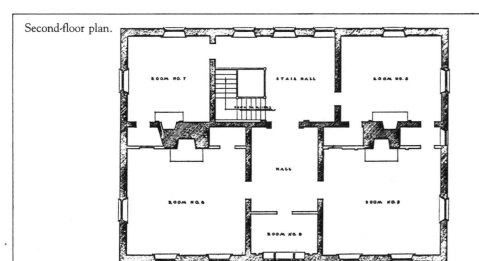

ROOM NO.7   STAIR HALL   ROOM NO.8

HALL

ROOM NO.6   ROOM NO.5

ROOM NO.8

First-floor plan.

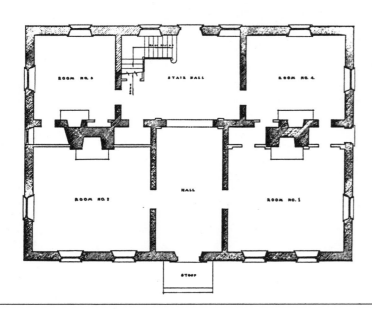

ROOM NO.3   STAIR HALL   ROOM NO.4

HALL

ROOM NO.2   ROOM NO.1

STOOP

North elevation.

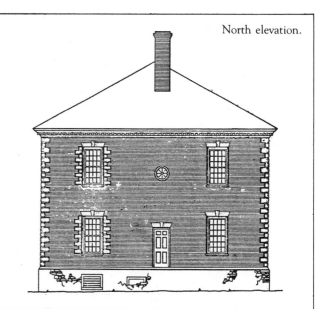

South elevation.

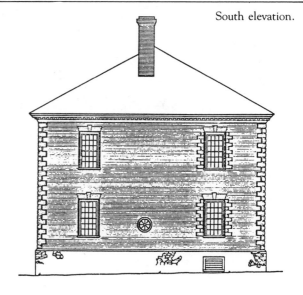

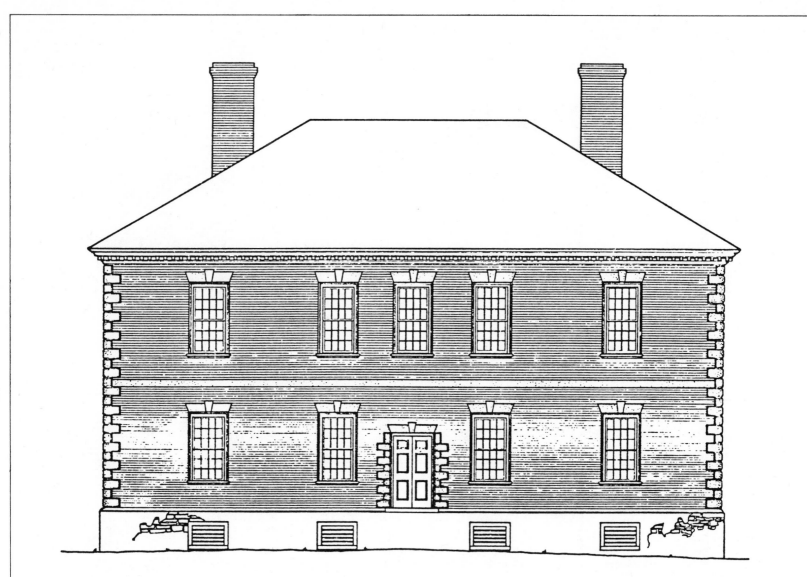

West (rear) elevation.

4. The Cliffs

Located in Philadelphia's Fairmount Park, The Cliffs is one of a number of eighteenth-century houses which were once considered fashionable country dwellings favored by the city's upper class. The Cliffs was built for a prominent Quaker merchant, Jonathan Fisher, in 1753, and was acquired by the park commission in 1868. Of stone construction, both the front and rear facades were stuccoed and rusticated. The ends remained untouched.

Various additions have been made to the house, including a dormer on the rear, a garage, and boiler room, but the essential form has remained intact. The original floor plan has been changed on at least the basement level. Here the space has been partitioned to include a den, laundry, bathroom, and pantry as well as the original kitchen. On the second floor, a bath has been added to the original plan.

From all exterior appearances, The Cliffs appears to be a typical Georgian Colonial, but it does not follow a center-hall plan. The main stairway is tucked away in one corner of the house, as it might have been in a less sophisticated dwelling of the same period. There is ample room, nevertheless, for converting the floor plans to introduce a center hall—if desired.

In other respects, The Cliffs is typically Georgian Colonial. The front entrance is matched exactly by a similarly designed entrance at the rear; the windows parallel each other front and rear. The east side of the house was altered at some time, two previous window openings having been stoned up. The opening that was closed on the east side now contains a dumbwaiter, a useful device when the kitchen is located a floor away from the dining room.

The paneled east wall of the dining room is well worth study. Included in it are raised panel doors which hide the dumbwaiter, stairs to the basement, and stairs to the second floor. At the far left of the space is also a narrow closet. In the center, of course, is a fireplace with a brick hearth extending before it.

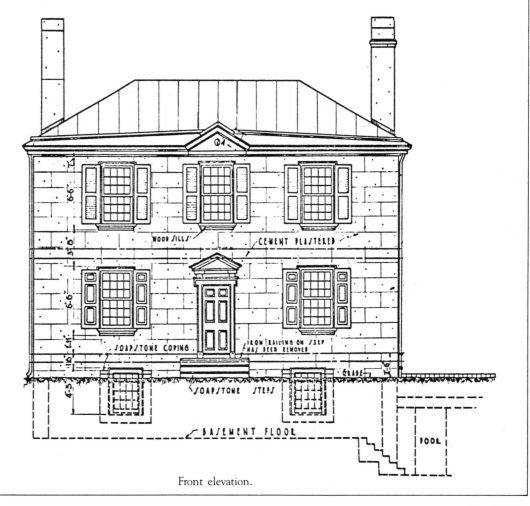

Front elevation.

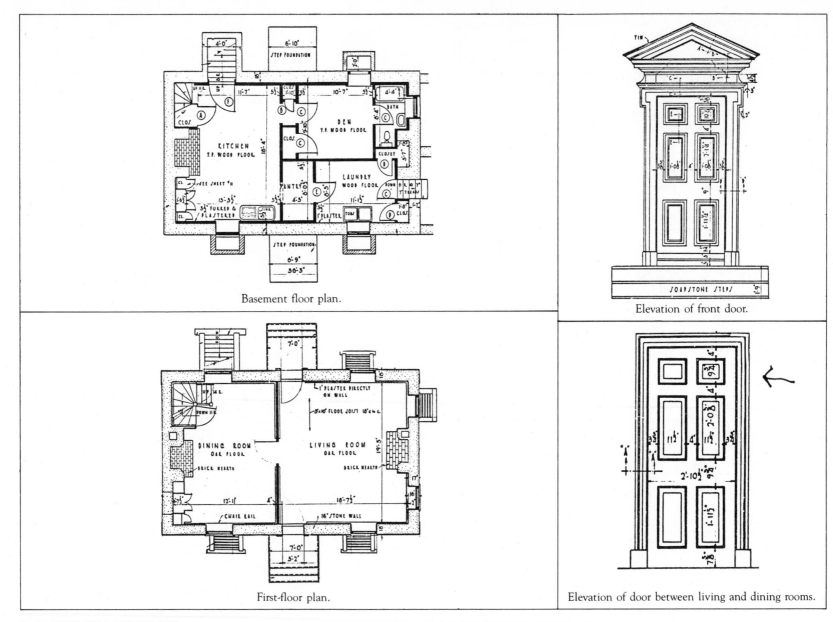

Basement floor plan.

First-floor plan.

Elevation of front door.

Elevation of door between living and dining rooms.

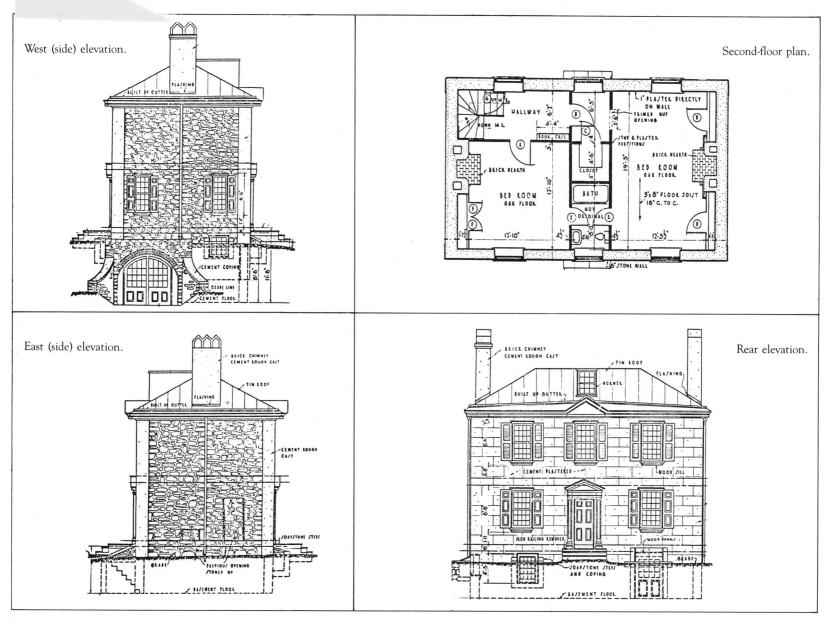

West (side) elevation.

Second-floor plan.

East (side) elevation.

Rear elevation.

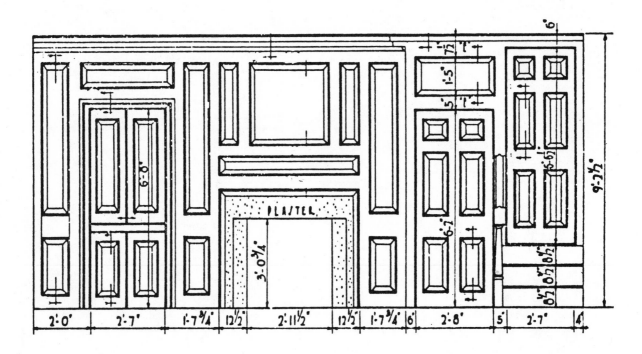

Elevation of east wall of dining room.

5. The Lindens

Originally located in Danvers, Massachusetts, The Lindens, built in 1754, was moved in its entirety to Washington, D.C., in the 1930s. It is easy to see why this house has been so prized and protected. It is high-style Georgian in almost every way. What is most remarkable about the house is the rusticated east or front facade which is composed entirely of wood blocks. Also striking is the central pedimented entrance with finely carved Corinthian pillars.

The Lindens is thought to have been designed by Peter Harrison, the architect of other important New England buildings of the period for Robert "King" Hooper. In the early 1930s, when these sketches were made, The Lindens had acquired a modern addition on one side which included a kitchen and bathrooms and which extended three floors. This is shown on the floor plans but not in the elevation drawings. The addition was removed when the house was relocated to Washington.

The floor plan is basically the same for each of the stories—a center hall from which branch the principal rooms: four on the first floor, four on the second, and seven small rooms on the third floor. The original kitchen appears to have been located on the first floor rather than in the basement, the latter location having gradually fallen out of favor for a kitchen during the second half of the eighteenth century. It was a great deal more convenient, of course, to both prepare and serve food on the same floor.

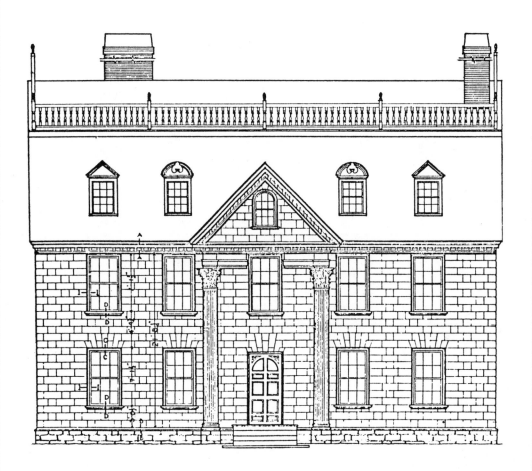

East (front) elevation.

West (rear) elevation.

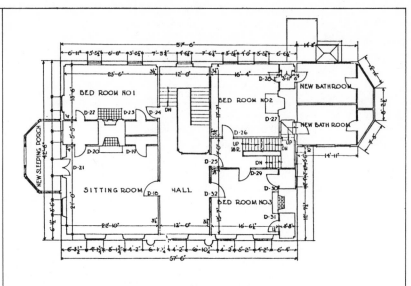

Second-floor plan.

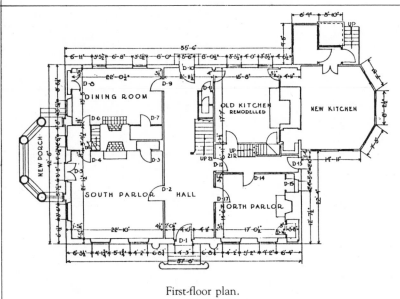

First-floor plan.

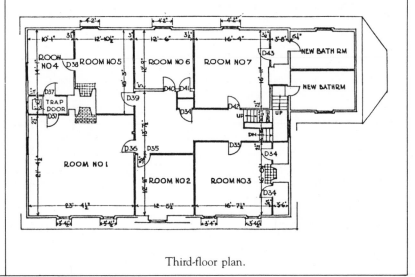

Third-floor plan.

South elevation.

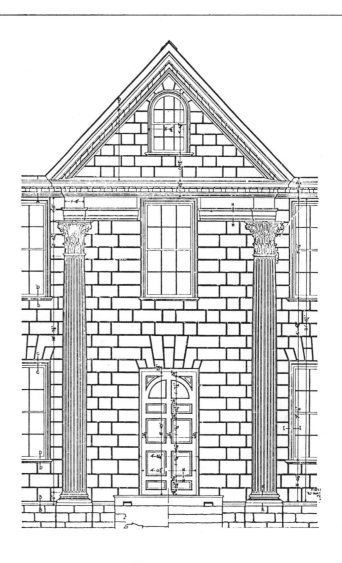

Main entrance.

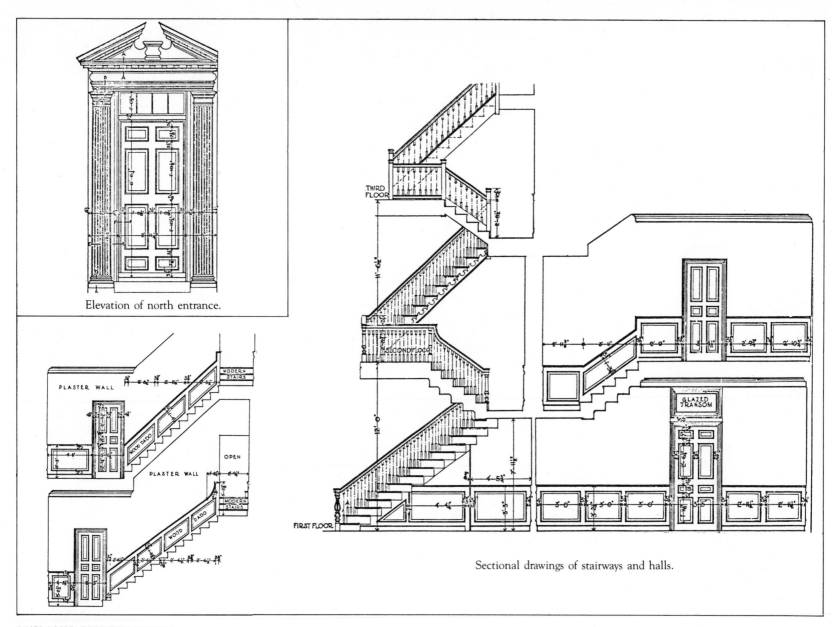

Elevation of north entrance.

Sectional drawings of stairways and halls.

6. Tate House

With its gambrel roof and center chimney, the Tate House in Portland, Maine, is typical of a northern New England Colonial house. Built in 1755, this is a dwelling with particularly handsome interior detailings, as the elevations of three dining room walls illustrate.

Because of the center chimney, the house has no central floor-through hall. Instead, there is a center front hall and a main staircase that climbs beside the chimney. The massive chimney is truly a multipurpose heating and cooking apparatus as it provides for two fireplaces, a cooking fireplace, and a baking oven on the first floor, three fireplaces on the second floor, and two fireplaces on the third floor.

All the major exterior architectural elements are handsomely proportioned. The window glass is all sized 8 by 10 inches, the windows on the first floor being 9 over 9; the second floor, 9 over 6; and the third floor, 6 over 6 or, on the sides, 9 over 6. The main entrance is defined by a pediment in the Georgian manner.

The dining room contains a handsome paneled wall, incorporating several features of note: a superbly pilastered fireplace, a built-in cupboard, and raised-panel wainscoting. Note that the building has been modernized with the addition of a bathroom wing to the rear on the first floor as well as a bath on the second. Neither of these improvements detract from the essential character of the house.

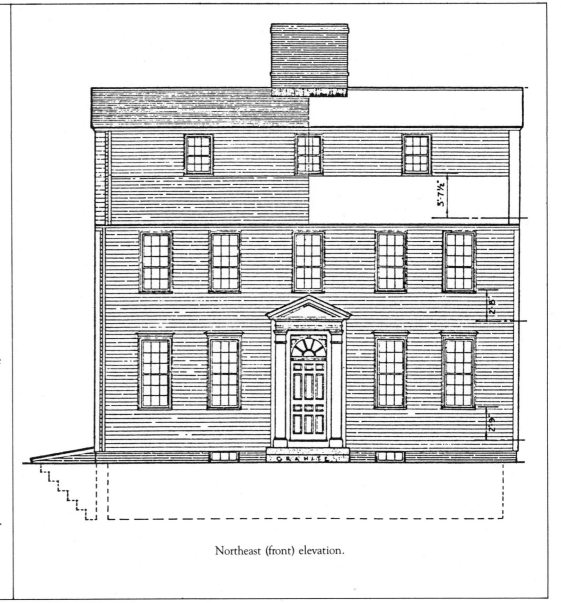

Northeast (front) elevation.

Southwest (rear) elevation.

Second-floor plan.

First-floor plan.

Third-floor plan.

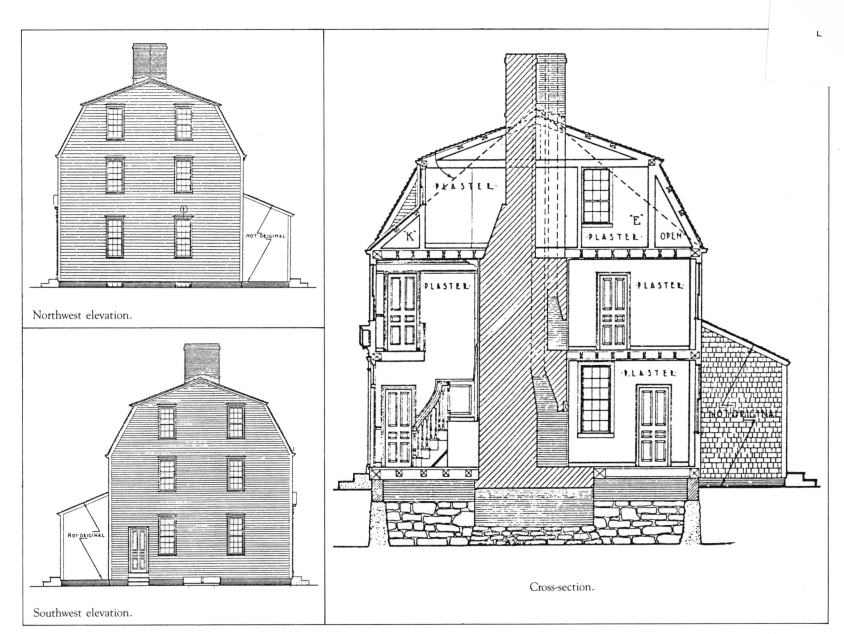

Northwest elevation.

Southwest elevation.

Cross-section.

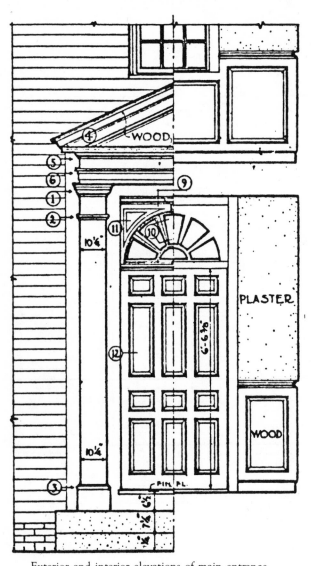

WOOD

PLASTER

WOOD

Exterior and interior elevations of main entrance.

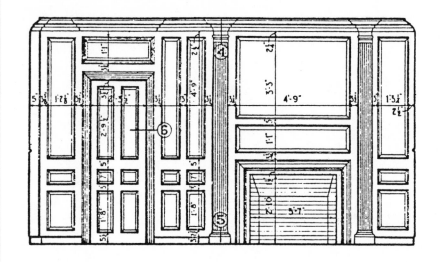

Elevations of dining room walls.

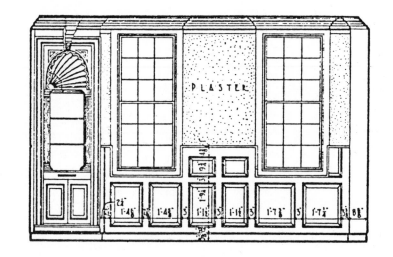

PLASTER

7. Jefferds Tavern

Like the Tate House in Portland, Jefferds Tavern has a central chimney and front hall. Unlike the former building, however, the tavern is a classic salt-box. The rear slanting portion of the building appears to have been part of the original c. 1760 house and not added later.

The building is entirely of wood construction. Even the roof is made up of wood shingles. The front entrance is a simple composition of pilasters and cornice which does justice to the straightforward lines of the house.

Jefferds Tavern was built for Captain Samuel Jefferds who was a tavernkeeper and mill owner in Wells, York County, Maine. To what extent the building was also used as a private residence is not known. The building was disassembled in 1939 and re-erected at the York Village Museum in 1942. The interior woodwork is particularly fine and has never been painted. As the elevations of the sitting room, dining room, and bedrooms show, closets with shelves were found throughout the house, a finding which contradicts the usual belief that early American dwellings were not well fitted with storage space. Perhaps use of the building as a tavern accounts for the difference.

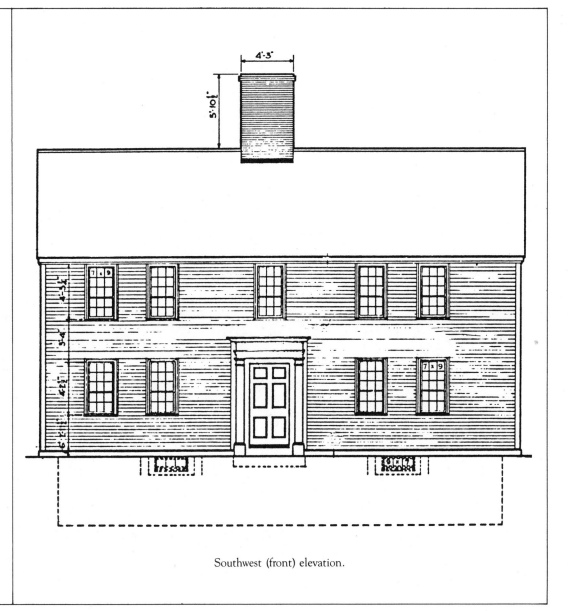

Southwest (front) elevation.

Northwest (rear) elevation.

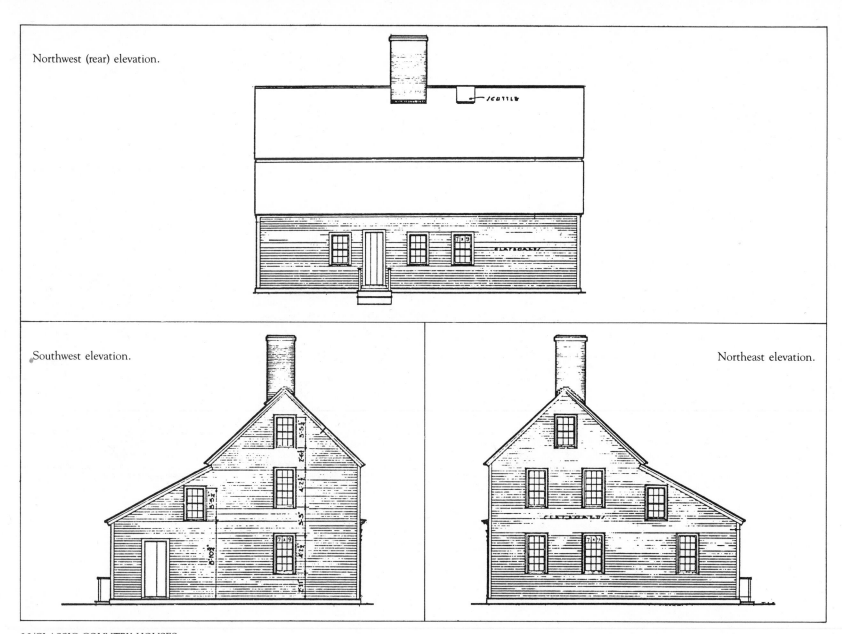

Southwest elevation.

Northeast elevation.

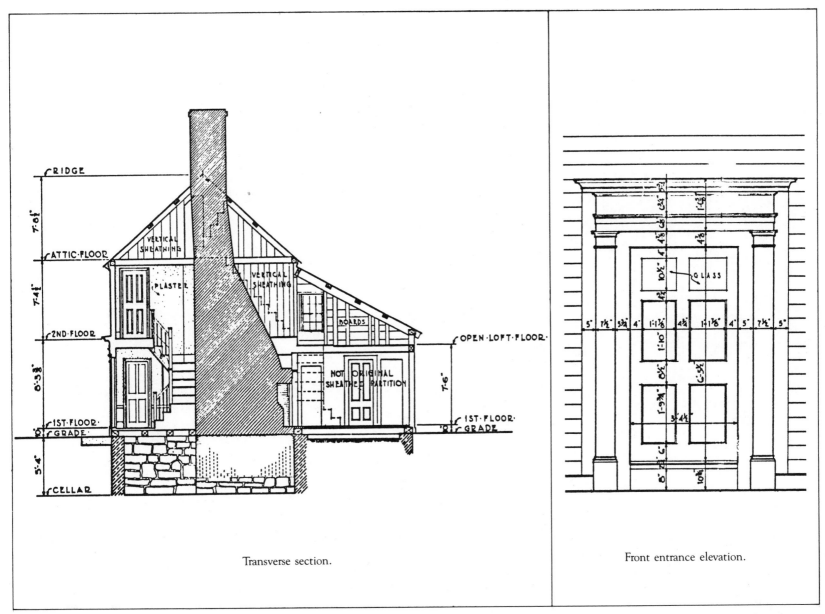

Transverse section.

Front entrance elevation.

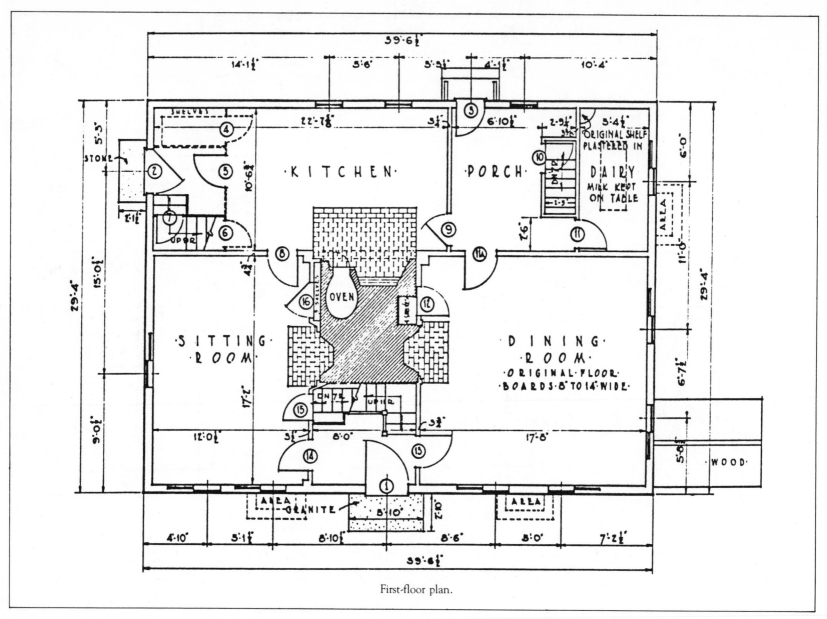

First-floor plan.

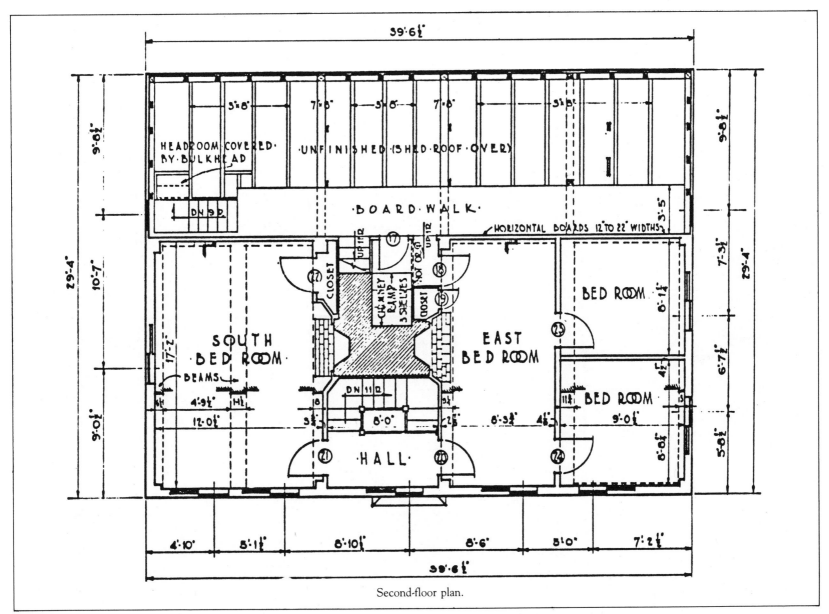

Second-floor plan.

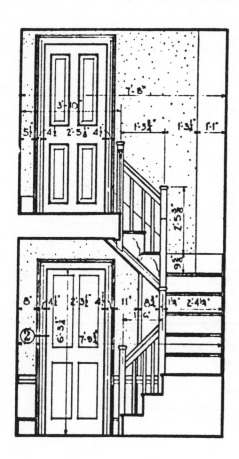

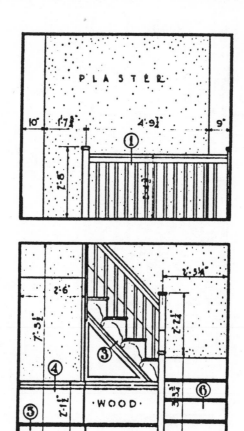

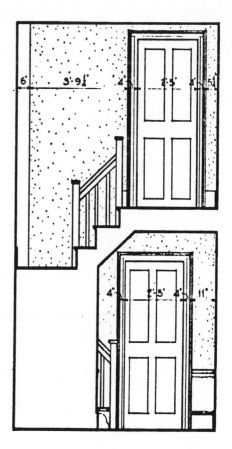

Elevations of stair hall.

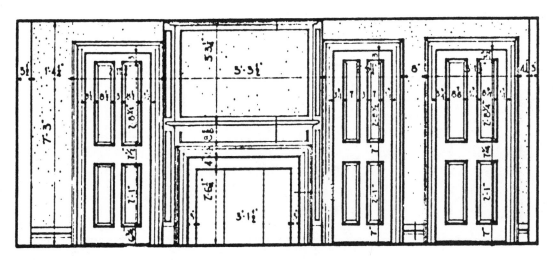

Elevation of northeast wall, sitting room.

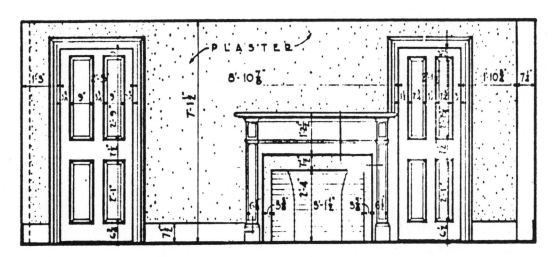

Elevation of southwest wall, dining room.

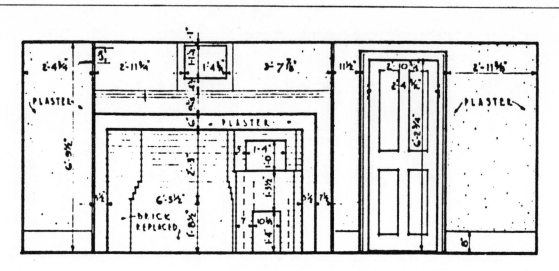

Elevation of southeast wall, kitchen.

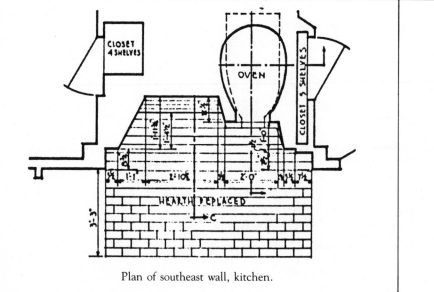

Plan of southeast wall, kitchen.

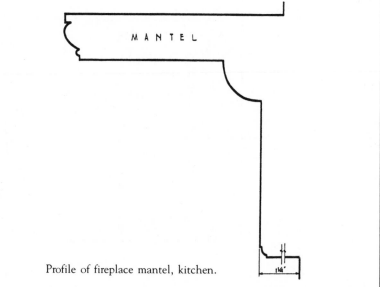

Profile of fireplace mantel, kitchen.

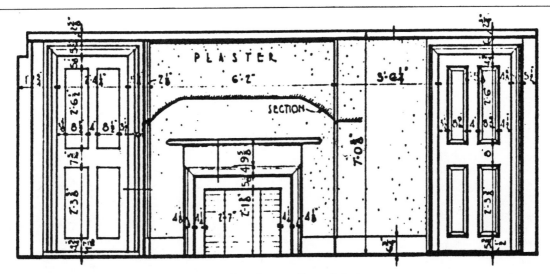

Elevation of northeast wall, south bedroom.

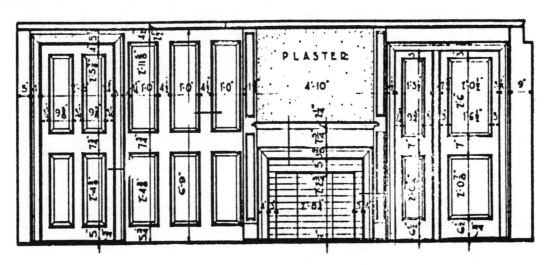

Elevation of southwest wall, east bedroom.

8. Bowman-Carney House

Gershom Flagg was the builder of this house, c. 1761, for Judge Jonathan Bowman. Located near Dresden, Maine, it was owned in the first half of the nineteenth century by James Carney, a blacksmith and shipbuilder. The hip-roofed house is noteworthy for its generously proportioned windows and doors. The windows on the second floor are as large as those on the first or principal floor.

A front porch was added to the house at a later time, but this has been removed in the facade drawings and floor plans. A wood shed on one side of the main block now serves as a kitchen, the old kitchen now used as the dining room. Bathrooms have been installed on both the first and second floors, making use of space at the side of one of the chimneys. The "old secret stairs" (shown on the first-floor plan) remain a mystery and appear to have been removed.

The front and rear entrances, exactly parallel to each other, are quite well matched, although the rear doorway includes the addition of a glass transom and the side pilasters are longer than those on the front of the house. It is curious that this rear entrance should be somewhat more imposing than the front.

The center hall is quite wide, measuring 9 feet, and the walls have raised dado panels; the doors are also of a raised panel design. All of the principal rooms have well executed wood cornices.

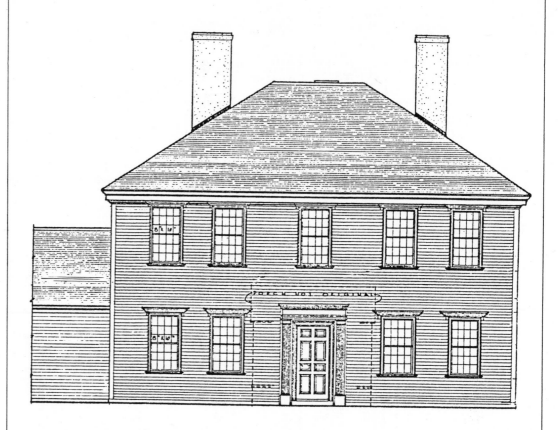

Northwest (front) elevation.

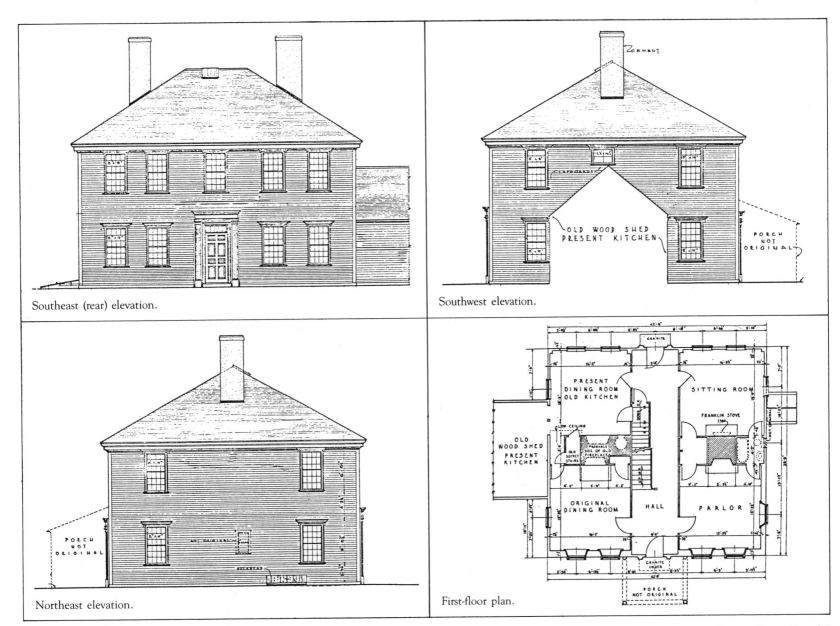

Southeast (rear) elevation.

Southwest elevation.

Northeast elevation.

First-floor plan.

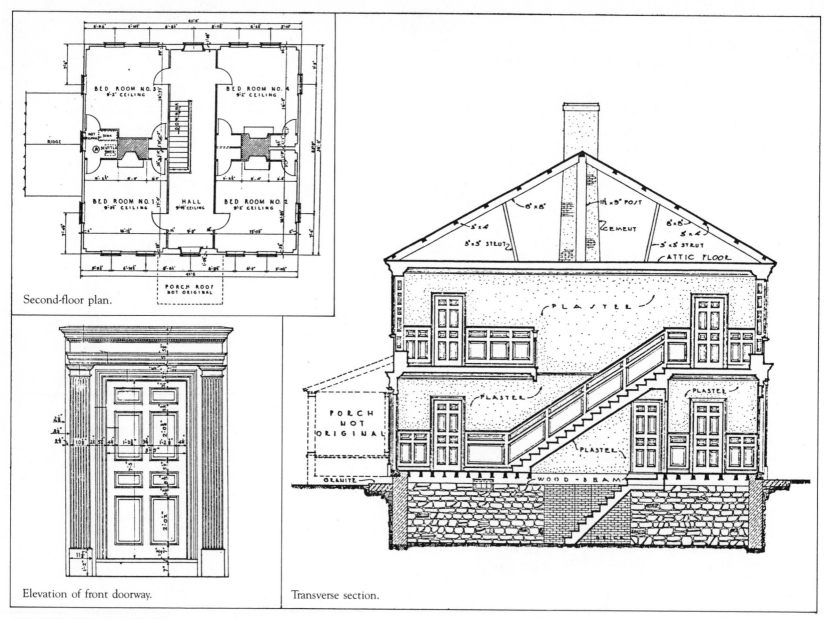

Second-floor plan.

Elevation of front doorway.

Transverse section.

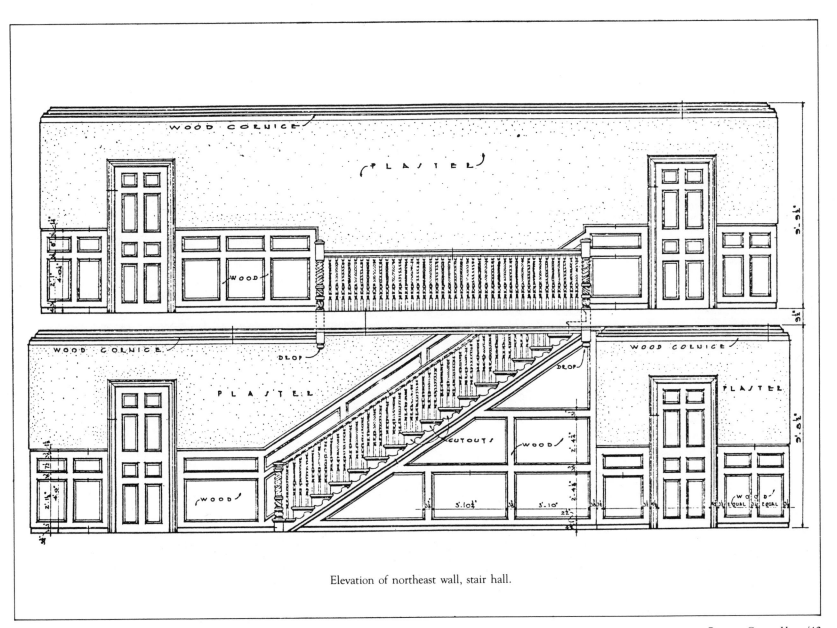

Elevation of northeast wall, stair hall.

9. Jarathmael Bowers House

Like The Lindens (see p. 23), the Bowers House has a rusticated wood block facade. And like that house, too, it has a gambrel roof. In common with most other Georgian Colonials, the Bowers House has a center hall from which four principal rooms radiate.

Built in 1770 in Somerset, Massachusetts, the residence was constructed in two sections. Differences in windows suggest that the rear portion, containing the kitchen, pantry, and several bedrooms, might be slightly older, but there is no documentary evidence to confirm this.

At one time there was a pediment over the main entrance. Where it existed is indicated in the drawings by dashes over the door. The front stoop is expansive, the steps progressing in two stages. In the 1930s, when these drawings were executed, the exterior walls were painted light yellow and the corners, brown. The front entrance and other trim was white.

As the plans and elevations of the north parlor show, the interior woodwork was very well executed. A wood dado of raised panels surrounds the room, and the fireplace wall is distinguished by handsome carved pilasters. The mantel dates from the nineteenth century, as probably does the marble fireplace facing.

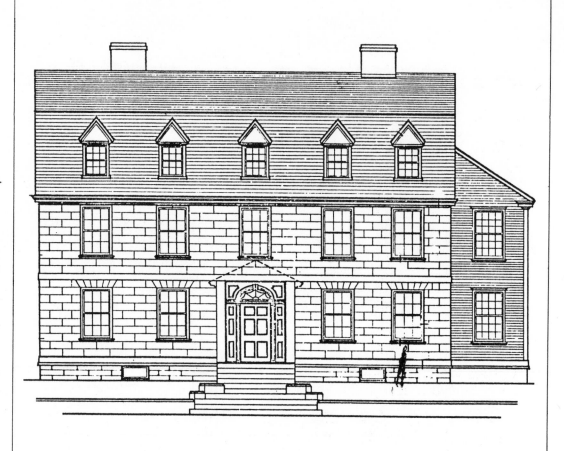

East (front) elevation.

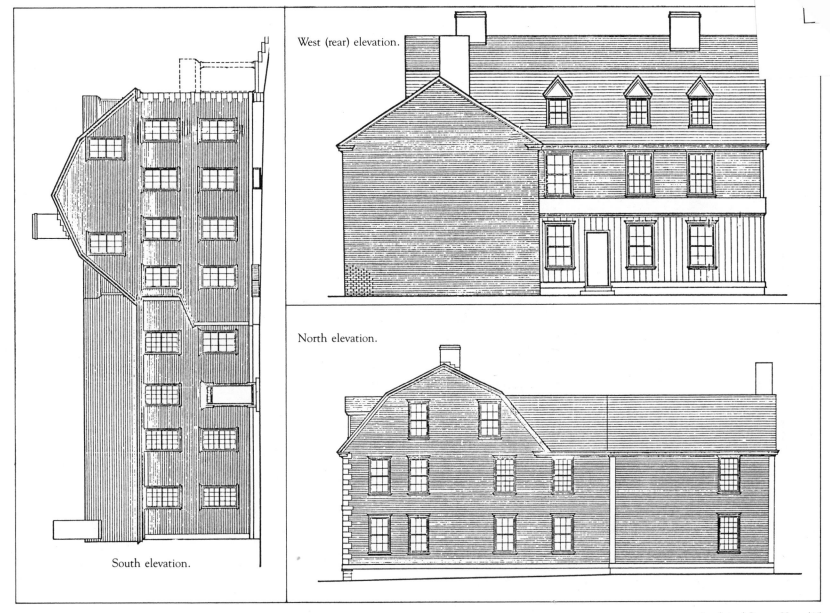

West (rear) elevation.

North elevation.

South elevation.

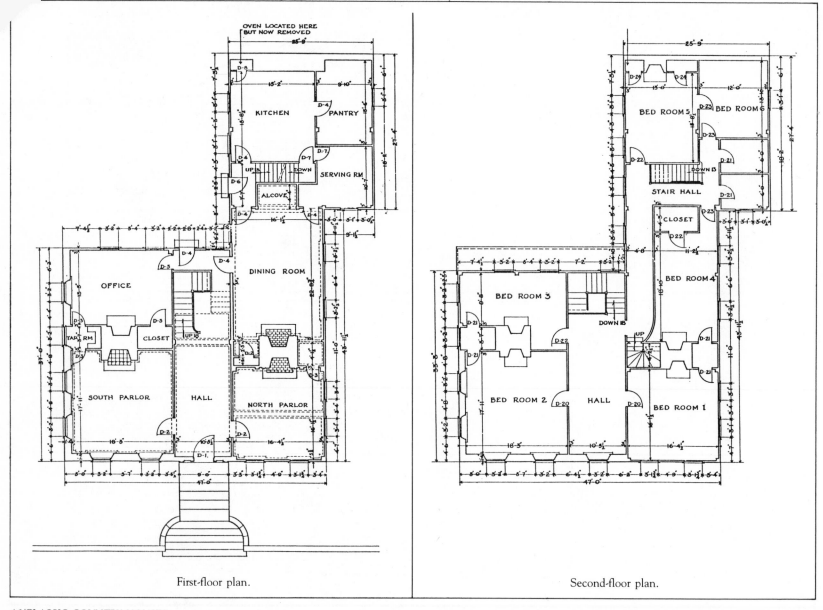

First-floor plan.

Second-floor plan.

Elevation of front entrance.

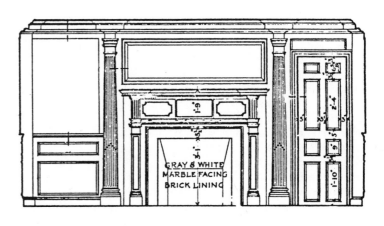

GRAY & WHITE
MARBLE FACING
BRICK LINING

Elevation of south wall, north parlor.

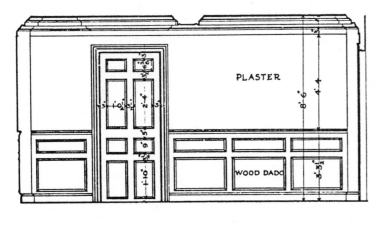

PLASTER

WOOD DADO

Elevation of west wall, north parlor.

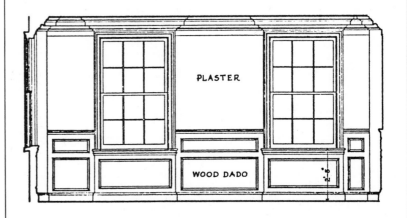

PLASTER

WOOD DADO

Elevation of east wall, north parlor.

10. Fort Hunter Mansion

A frontier garrison north of Harrisburg, Pennsylvania, dating from the 1720s, was the site chosen by Archibald McAllister in the 1780s for his country mansion. A very imposing structure of stone, Fort Hunter Mansion consists of three sections—the front three-story mansion house, a two-room-deep stone extension, and a one-room-deep wood frame extension. Whether all three units date from the 1780s is not known. Differences in the windows between the front and middle sections would seem to suggest an earlier date for the latter.

Certain decorative exterior architectural elements are not original. The wooden front porch and steps, for example, were added later. It is probable that the wooden cornice brackets are also nineteenth century additions. The main entrance and the fine Palladian window above it, however, are very much of the Georgian period. So, too, are the paneled shutters.

The stone extension has attractive two-story verandas on both sides. The woodwork suggests that they, too, were additions of the 1800s. Rooms "E" and "D" of this section were once one large room.

The mansion is now a house museum and the rooms, especially in the front section of the house, are particularly attractive in ornamentation. There are only three principal rooms on the first floor of the section, but each is supplied with a fireplace and is amply proportioned. The main staircase is semicircular and gracefully occupies the center hall.

The four principal bedrooms on the second floor are each supplied with a fireplace, these being angled in a way to make the best possible use of the chimney at each end of the house. The room designated "L" on the second-floor plan was probably a sitting or sewing room. Behind the main section are secondary living and service areas such as the kitchen, pantry, laundry, and servants' bedrooms.

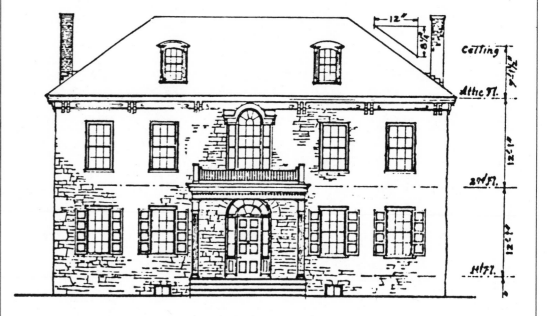

South (front) elevation.

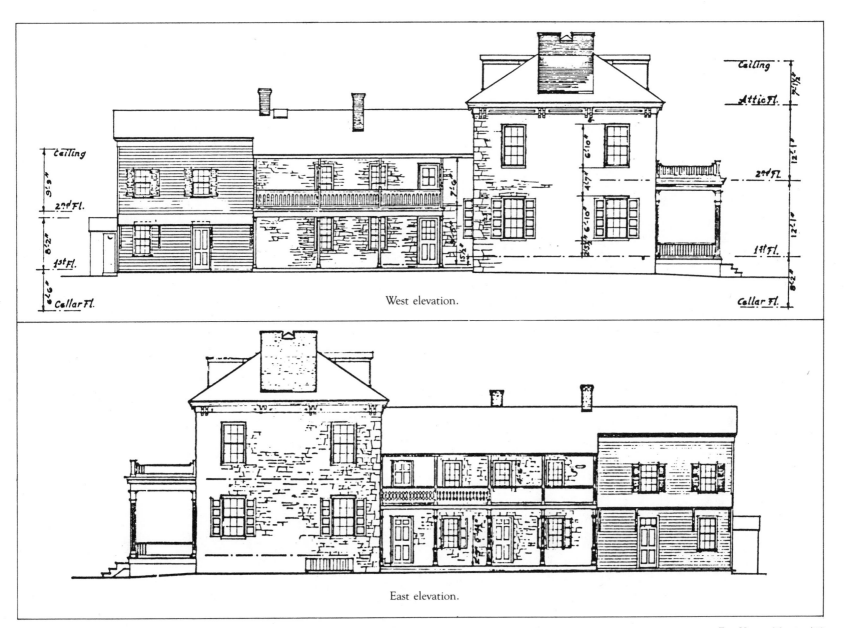

West elevation.

East elevation.

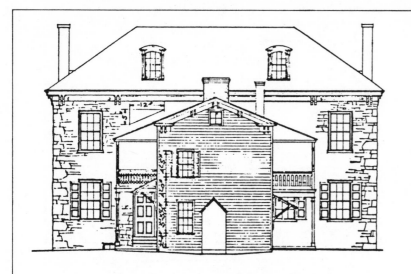

North (rear) elevation.

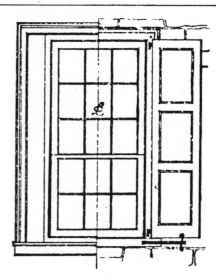

Exterior and interior details, typical window in front section.

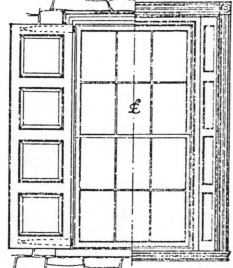

Exterior and interior details, typical window in middle section.

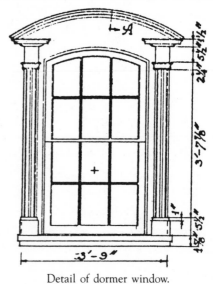

Detail of dormer window.

First-floor plan.

Second-floor plan.

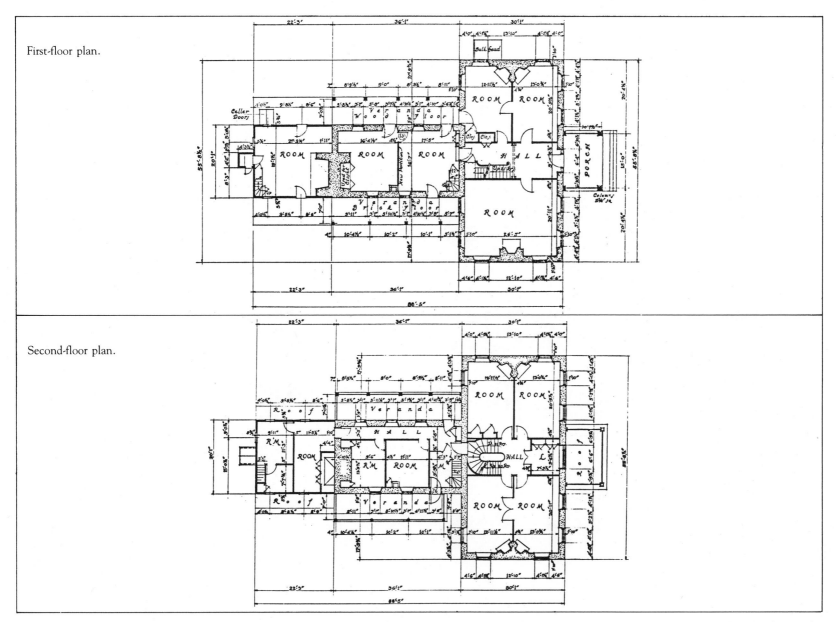

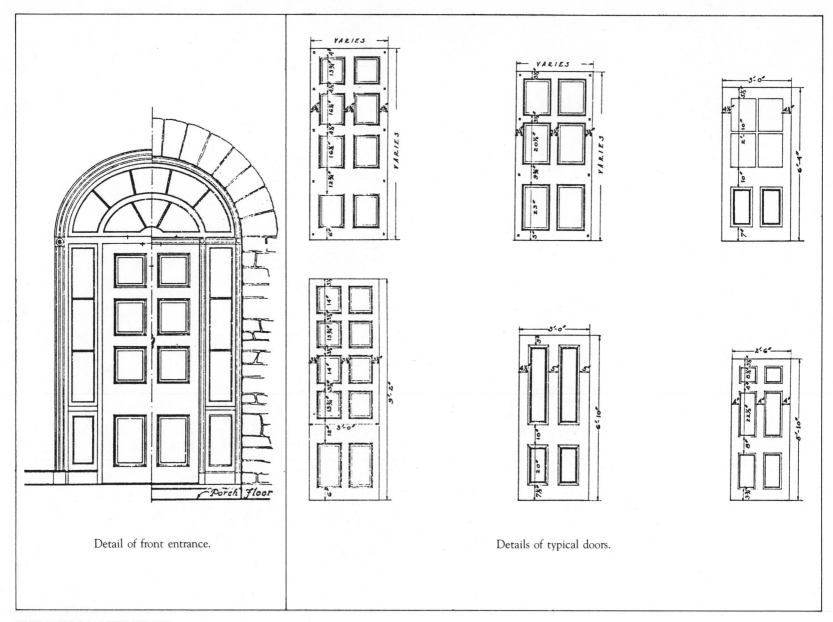

Detail of front entrance.

Details of typical doors.

11. Rock Ford

Built for the Revolutionary War adjutant general of the Army, Edward Hand, between 1783 and 1793, Rock Ford is now a house museum. Located in the vicinity of Lancaster, Pennsylvania, the house has been meticulously restored in recent years. Of brick construction, it has the usual center hall floor plan found in most Georgian Colonial houses.

The exterior and interior detailing of this house is particularly noteworthy and is especially visible in the front entrance and the wall decoration of the principal rooms. Like many tidewater Virginia homes, Rock Ford is built on a basement which is partially above ground level. The kitchen and pantry are found on this floor as is space for other service functions. The west elevation shows the basement level as being almost fully exposed.

There are four principal rooms on each floor, and a small sitting or sewing room included at the end of the hall on the second floor. The third-floor rooms are somewhat smaller since they are tucked under the gable roof. Each top-floor room has one window; there are no dormers.

Two chimneys serve as many as eleven fireplaces, the largest being the cooking fireplace in the basement. As seen in the elevation of the northwest first-floor room, there is no mantel but, rather, a shelf over the fireplace. The fireplace opening is framed in the same manner as the doors and cupboards. The fireplace in the southwest first-floor room has an overmantel or chimney breast in addition to a shelf.

North (front) elevation.

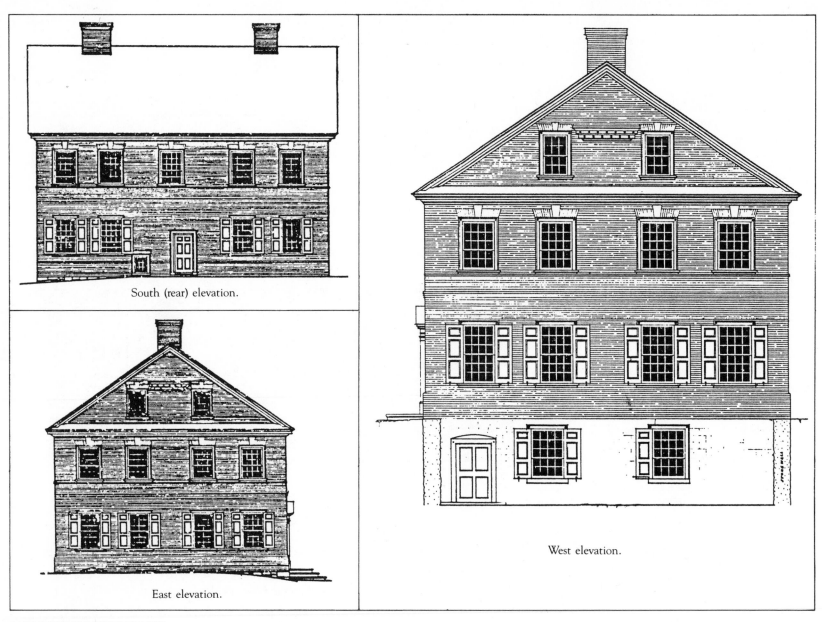

South (rear) elevation.

East elevation.

West elevation.

First-floor plan.

Third-floor plan.

Second-floor plan.

Basement floor plan.

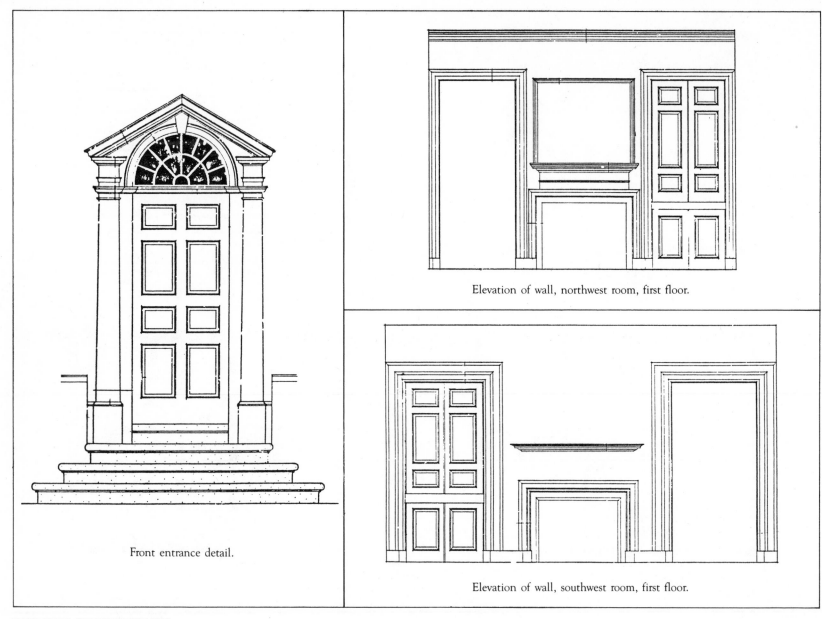

Front entrance detail.

Elevation of wall, northwest room, first floor.

Elevation of wall, southwest room, first floor.

12. Coleman-Hollister House

The design of this 1796 house located in Greenfield, Massachusetts, reflects the transition in style from the Georgian Colonial to the Federal. The changes can be seen in the use of pillared porches on each side of the front of the house, in the decorative wall plaques, and the dining room bay. The basic plan of the front portion of the building, however, remains very much the same as it would have been earlier in the century with a center hall from which radiate four rooms on each of the two main floors. Some of the decorative exterior elements date from the 1850s; these include the leaded glass windows, the south porch, and the pediments over the first-story windows on the south side.

The main staircase is an exceptionally graceful feature, and allowance for the stair's wide spiral is made in the rear hall. A more commonplace set of stairs is located immediately behind the main hall off the kitchen. The kitchen wing also dates from the 1850s. Note that it does not contain a cooking fireplace. Undoubtedly it was equipped with a flue so that a stove of some sort could be used. Where the kitchen was originally located is not known, but it may have been in the basement.

Two chimneys are centered on each side of the house and serve fireplaces in five rooms. Rather than a sewing or sitting room on the front side of the second floor, there is an alcove from which two closets have been carved. Other rooms on the second story are also liberally supplied with closets, probably additions of the 1850s. There is even a bathroom tucked into the rear, later section of the house.

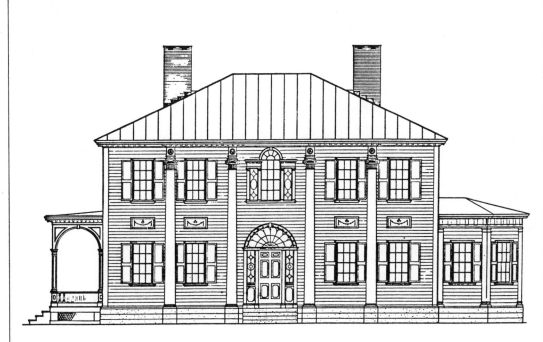

Front elevation.

South elevation.

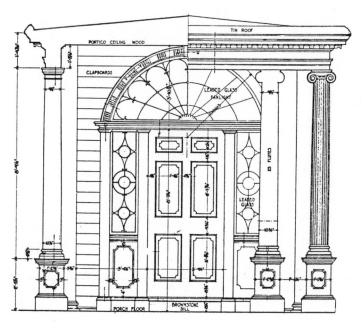

Elevation of front entrance and portico.

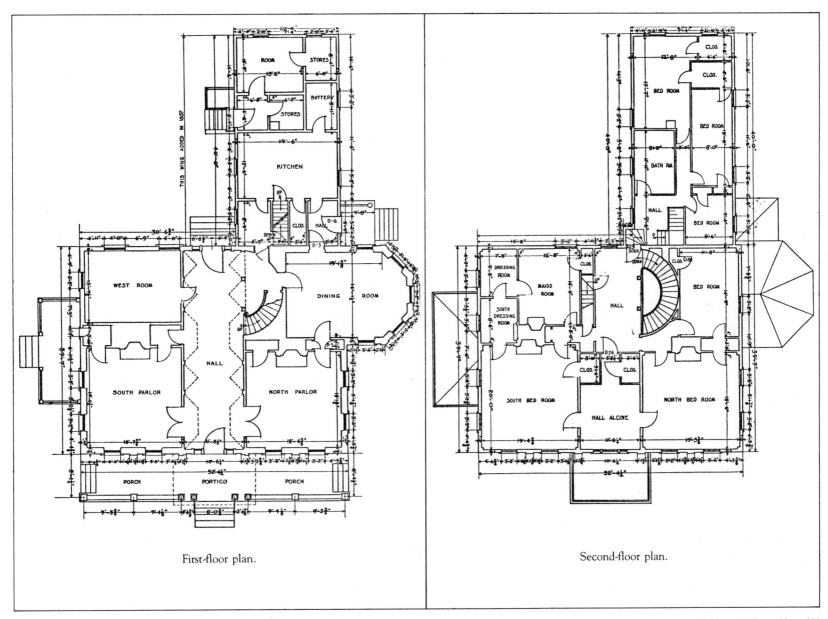

First-floor plan.

Second-floor plan.

Details of Palladian window.

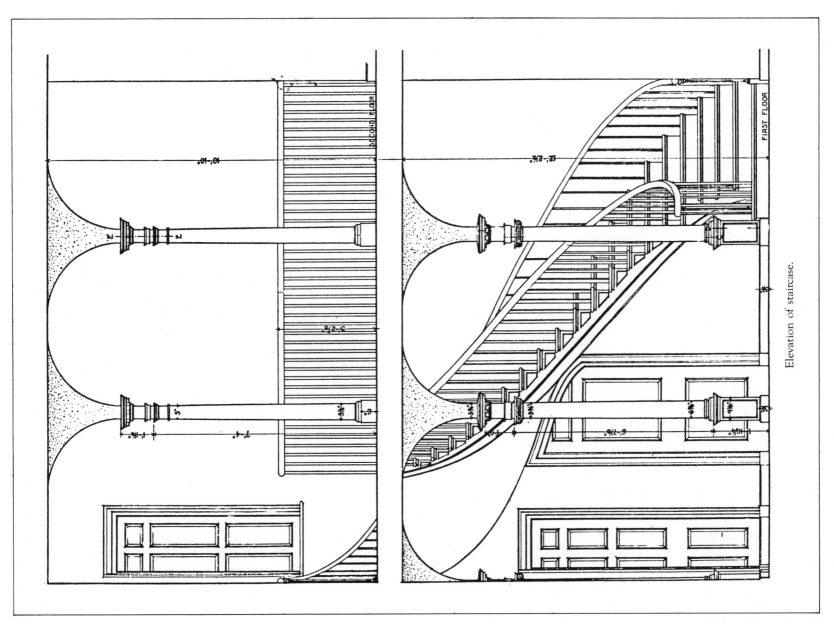

Elevation of staircase.

13. Marshall House

Captain Thomas Marshall, brother of John Marshall, the famous Chief Justice of the United States Supreme Court, built this two-story brick mansion between 1798 and 1800 in Washington, Kentucky. The Marshall family of Virginia included numerous illustrious sons, most of whom moved in the 1780s to the Kentucky frontier. Before the main brick block was built, there was only a small one-story frame section. It now houses the kitchen.

Marshall House is a modest house for its time, being barely more than one-room deep. A parlor occupies all of one side of the first floor; the other half is divided into a dining room and a sitting room. A center hall separates the two sections. The second floor contains four bedrooms and a dressing room, and most of these rooms are small. The third floor contains a particularly gruesome set of rooms labeled on the floor plan as "refractory slave quarters" and divided into a "cell room" and "punishment room."

Marshall House was built in the Federal style, the exterior windows being capped with stone lintels and the main entrance door with a fanlight. The sidelights are an addition of the 1840s.

The interior decoration is very simple and neoclassical in spirit. All of the woodwork was originally painted white. The parlor has a plastered cornice and ceiling decoration, and there is wainscoting in the main hall. Chair rails are used in other rooms. Fireplaces are provided for all the first-story rooms and for three of the four second-story bedrooms.

West (front) elevation.

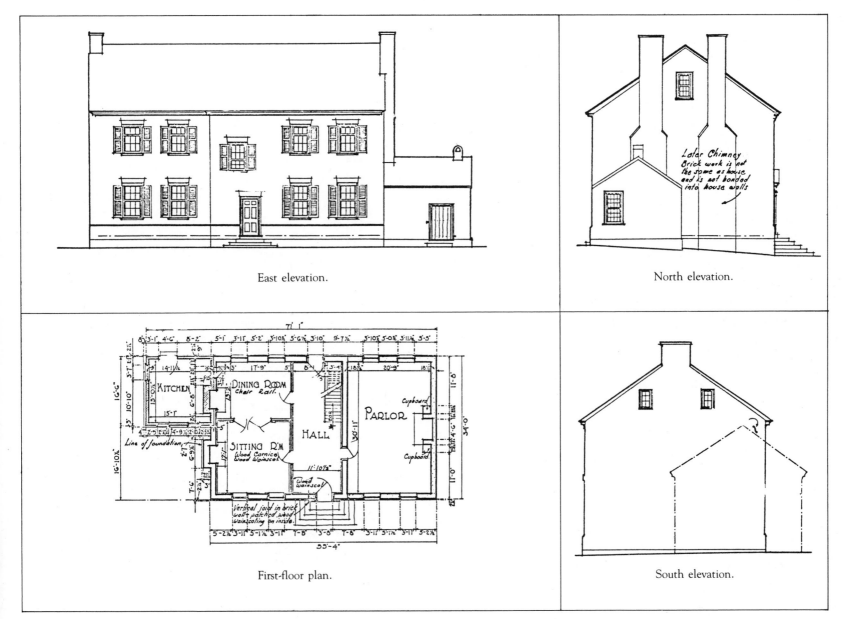

East elevation.

North elevation.

Later Chimney Brick work is not the same as house and is not bonded into house walls

First-floor plan.

KITCHEN

DINING ROOM
Chair Rail.

HALL

PARLOR

Cupboard

SITTING R'M
Wood Cornice
Wood Wainscot

Cupboard

Line of foundation.

Wood Wainscot

Vertical joint in brick wall, patched wood wainscoting on inside.

South elevation.

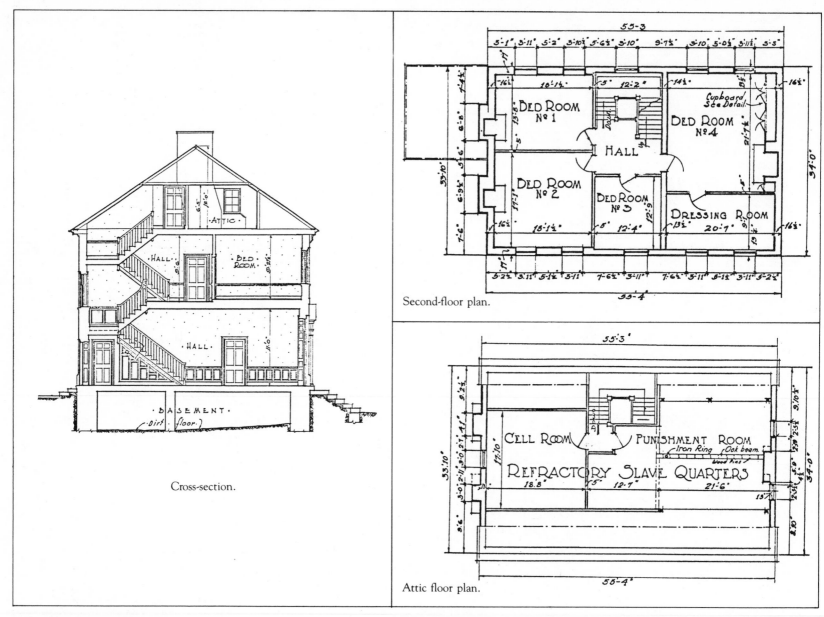

Cross-section.

Second-floor plan.

Attic floor plan.

14. Musterfield House

Built in 1805 in Clarksburg, Massachusetts, Musterfield House is distinguished by its prominent pilasters and pedimented entrance. The building has undergone some reconstruction over the years. The west wing, originally only one story, was moved in the 1880s from the rear of the building to the west side.

The floor plans indicate that there are two kitchens, the original one in the main block. It is equipped with a fireplace. The new kitchen in the wing is fitted with a flue for a stove.

Although simple in its center hall plan, Musterfield House nevertheless includes some unusual features. One is the second-story ballroom which stretches 42 feet across the front of the building. It is served by two fireplaces, both of which have since been bricked up. A second special feature is a secret closet hidden under stairs off one of the second-floor bedrooms. It was entered by removing a stair tread. Since the house was built in rural Berkshire County at a time when it was still a frontier area, such a hiding place was probably considered necessary. A third unusual element is the porch pediment. The panel is painted with a landscape, perhaps the work of an itinerant artist.

South elevation.

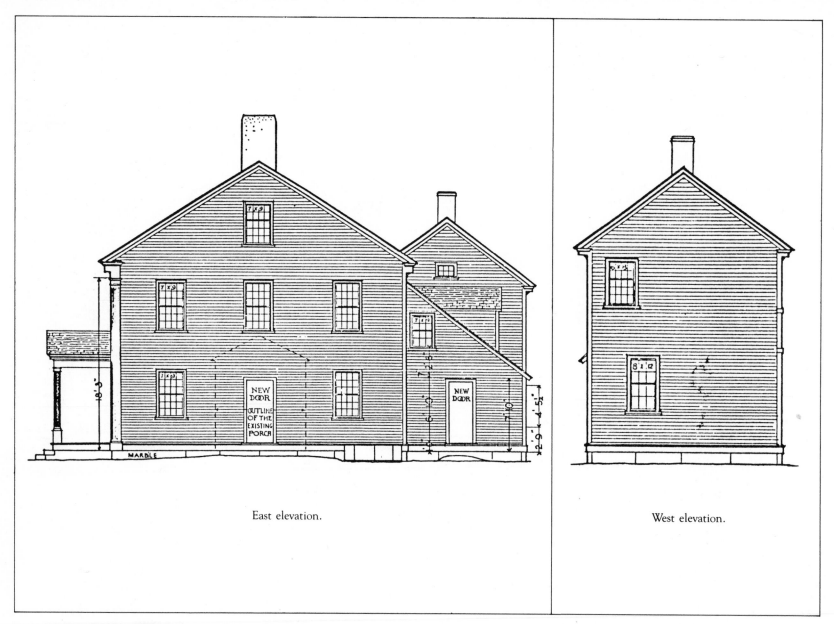

East elevation.

West elevation.

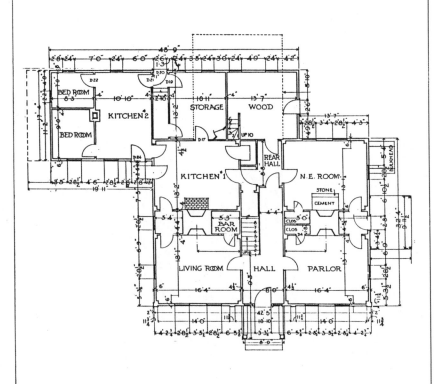

First-floor plan.

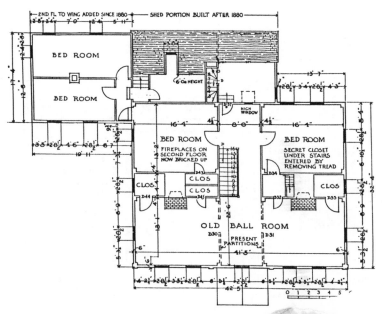

Second-floor plan.

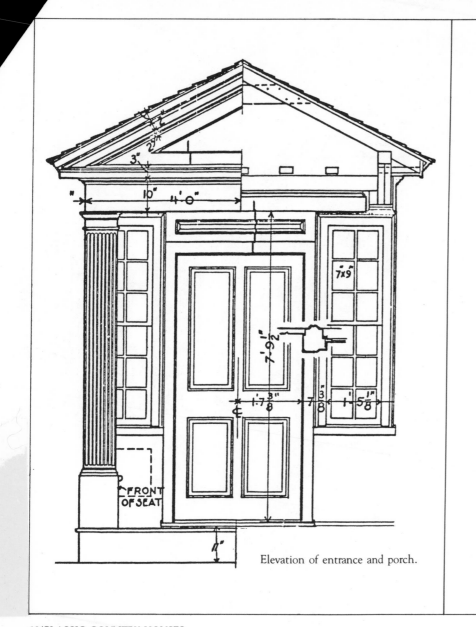

Elevation of entrance and porch.

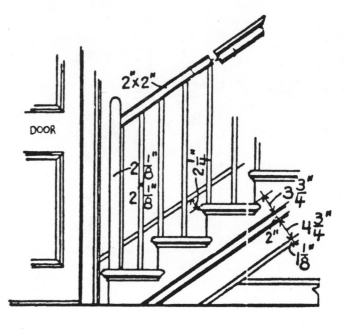

Stair details.

15. Moorhead House

The five-bay brick home of the Moorhead
family in Erie County, Pennsylvania, is a
traditional center-hall Colonial. Built in 1805
as a tavern, it incorporates some Federal-style
detailing of its time such as the sandstone
window heads and sills, and the main entrance with sidelights. Later additions include
the Colonial Revival side porch and front
portico, and the rear service wing.

The 18′ by 33′ space designated as the "living
room" on the floor plan would have served as
a spacious tap room. Across the hall are two
other rooms separated by sliding closet doors.
The kitchen was probably located on the partially above-ground basement level before the
addition of the rear wing.

Chimneys were built in the gable ends of
the building to serve seven fireplaces, one of
which has been bricked up. The second floor
is broken into four almost evenly-spaced rooms,
and in recent times provision has been made
for bathrooms. There is also a third, or attic,
floor with windows at each gable end.

North (front) elevation.

East elevation.

West elevation.

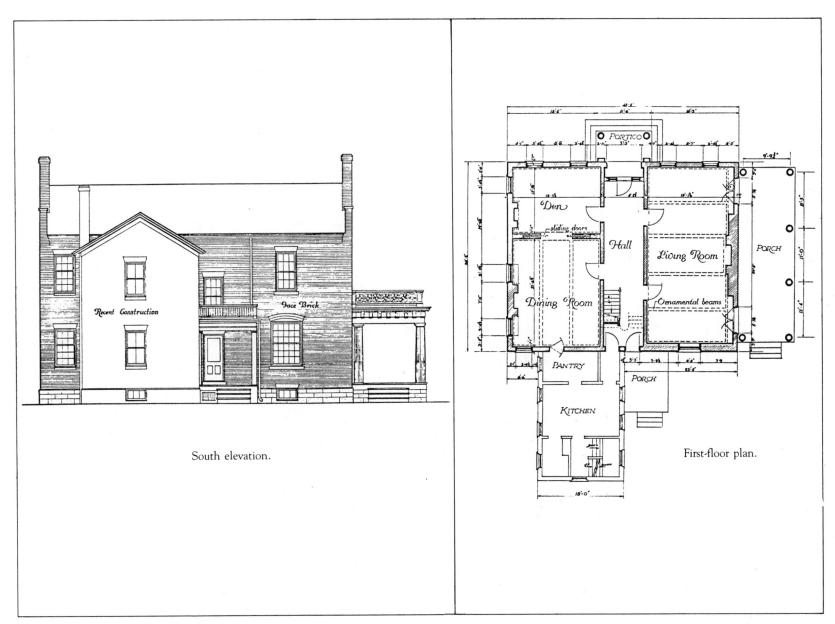

South elevation.

First-floor plan.

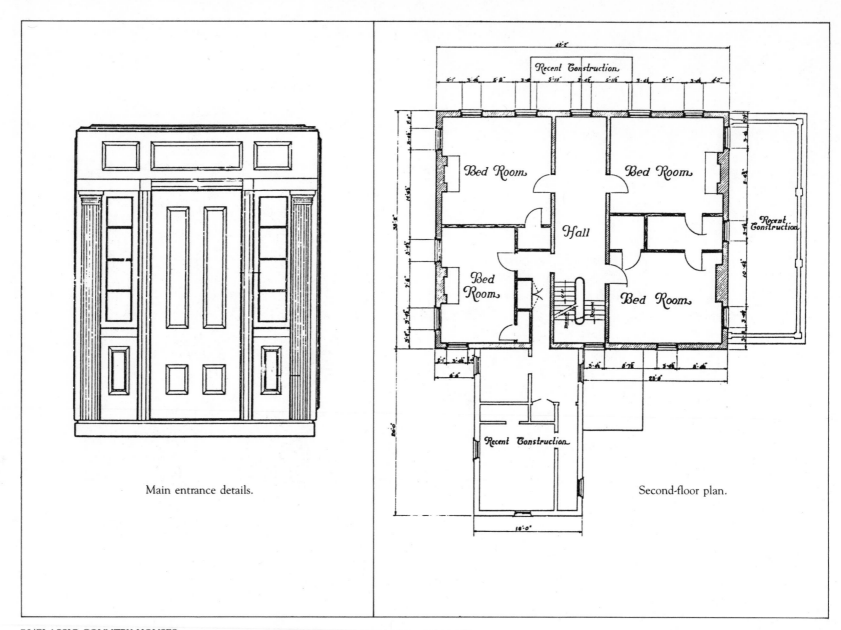

Main entrance details.

Second-floor plan.

16. Shoemaker House (Elm Lawn)

Elm Lawn is a very sophisticated house for a fairly remote location—Luzerne County in northeastern Pennsylvania. Built in 1820, the building is virtually a textbook example of a late-Colonial house. Its most obvious features are a second-story Palladian window, entryway with fanlight and sidelights, a two-room-deep center-hall floor plan, and a gable roof with chimneys at each end.

The rear service wing is also found on many similiar houses of the early 1800s. The wide overhang of the roof of this section, which incorporates a second-story galley porch, is typical of many early houses built in Pennsylvania, Maryland, Virginia, and Kentucky.

Although there have been some changes in the roof line over the years as well as alterations in windows and doors, Elm Lawn appears to have been built as one piece. The front section is a 46′ by 37′ box divided almost precisely into four equal rooms. These, of course, are separated by a wide center stair hall which also leads back to the rear service wing. This section of the house has been changed more than the other as it now includes two modern bathrooms on the second floor.

The interior woodwork is representative of that found in many early nineteenth-century houses. Corner blocks and a series of fluted moldings define windows and doors; wood fireplace mantels are compositions of pilasters and an entablature with centerpiece and corner posts.

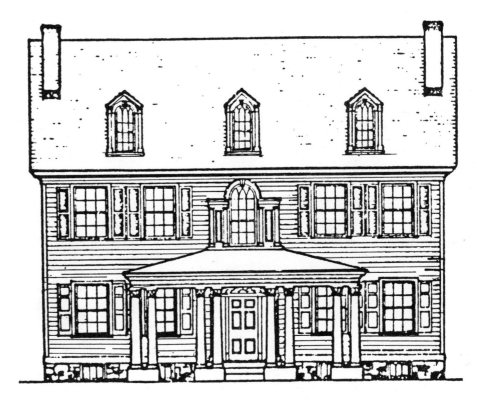

Northwest (front) elevation.

Northeast elevation.

Southwest elevation.

Southeast (rear) elevation.

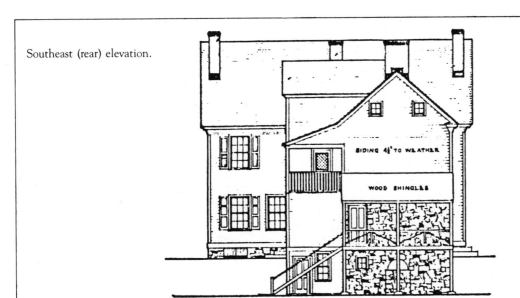

SIDING 4½" TO WEATHER

WOOD SHINGLES

South front bedroom fireplace mantel.

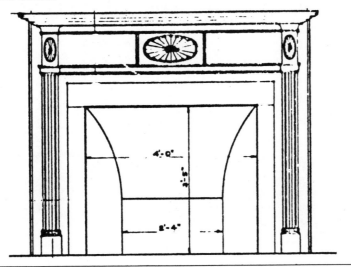

4'-0"

2'-4"

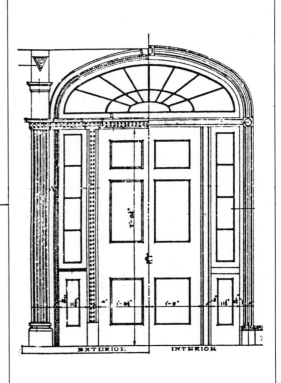

EXTERIOR   INTERIOR

Front entrance.

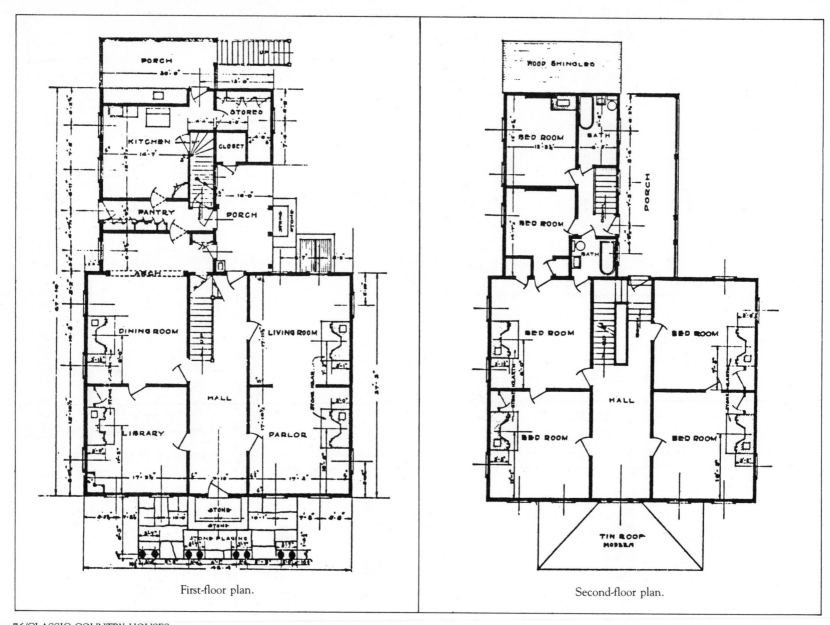

First-floor plan.

Second-floor plan.

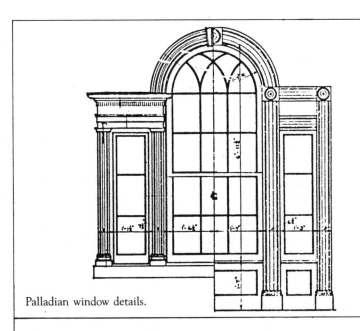

Palladian window details.

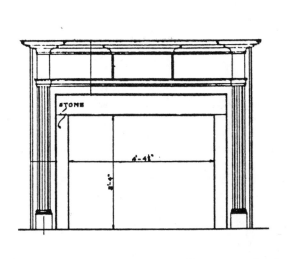

Dining room fireplace mantel.

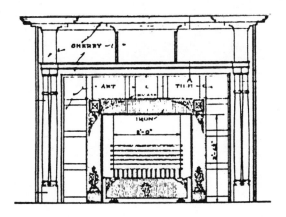

Library fireplace mantel.

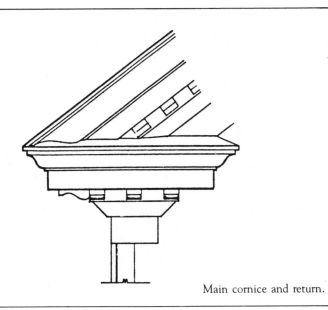

Main cornice and return.

17. Mount Nebo

The style of Mount Nebo, built near Milledgeville, Georgia, in 1823, is variously described as Federal or Jeffersonian Classicism. The latter term is also applied to houses built in the Old South which center on a two-story pavilion with a full-width one- or two-story columned portico. The semicircular Roman arch is used liberally in windows and doors, as here, and the Tuscan order may be employed for columns along with borrowed Greek orders.

Mount Nebo handsomely displays both Roman Doric and Ionic columns in its two-story portico. The semicircular arch is shown in the fanlight of the main entrance, the second-story porch door, and in the sunburst applied to the pediment panel. The dormer windows are also round-headed.

The front entrance is distinguished by its unusual double doors; the second-floor front porch door is identical in design, but of one piece. The wooden columns are also of one piece. The entablature between the two porch floors was originally of wood but was covered with galvanized iron after 1850.

Mount Nebo is unusual in having five chimneys, two attached to each gable end and a fifth rising alongside the center pavilion. Each principal room is served by a fireplace. Exactly where the kitchen was located is not known; it may have been in a separate building or rear wing. The pantry is found in a rear northwest corner room. This room, a porch, and an office are all attached to the main block of the building as a salt-box extension.

The front reception and rear stair halls are particularly handsome. A very graceful arch delineates the passage between the two areas. The stairs are designed in a wide, graceful spiral.

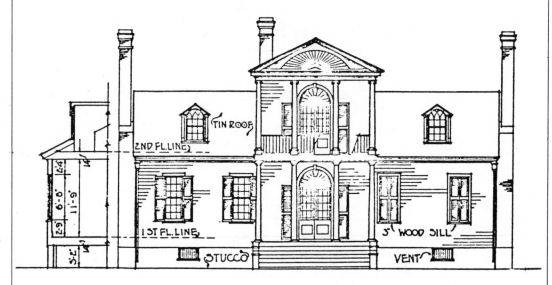

South (front) elevation.

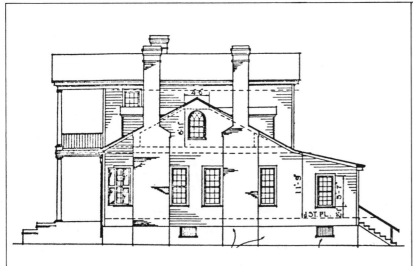

East elevation.

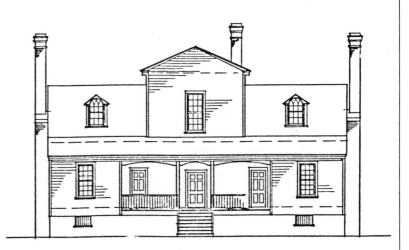

North (rear) elevation.

West elevation.

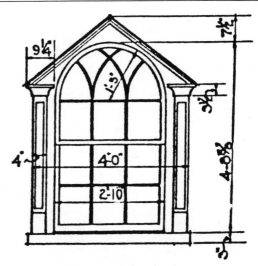

Dormer window detail.

Front porch detail.

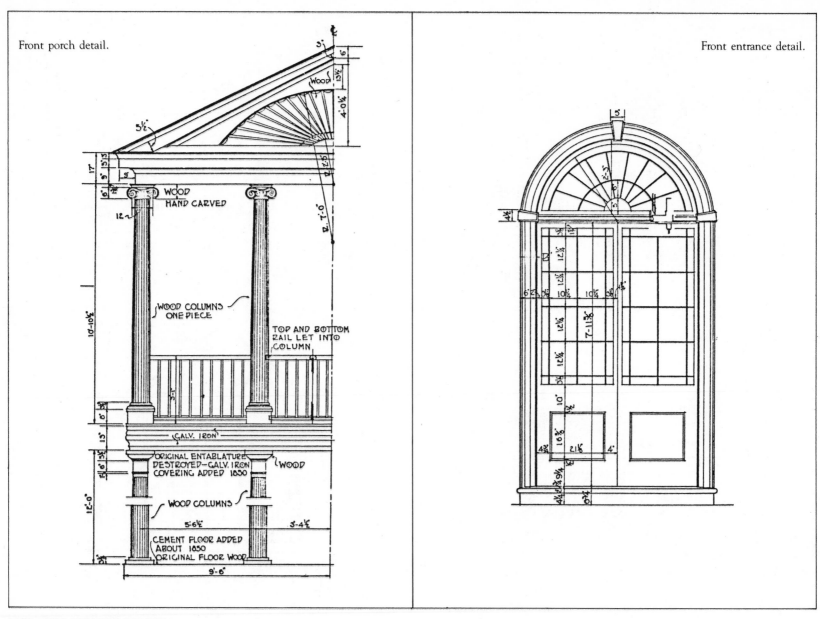

WOOD
HAND CARVED

WOOD COLUMNS
ONE PIECE

TOP AND BOTTOM
RAIL LET INTO
COLUMN

GALV. IRON

ORIGINAL ENTABLATURE
DESTROYED—GALV. IRON
COVERING ADDED 1850

WOOD

WOOD COLUMNS

CEMENT FLOOR ADDED
ABOUT 1850
ORIGINAL FLOOR WOOD

Front entrance detail.

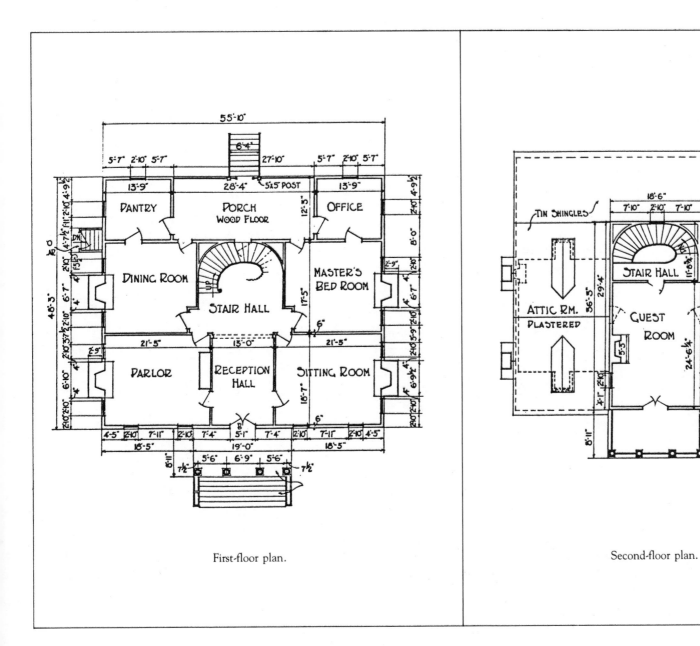

First-floor plan.

Second-floor plan.

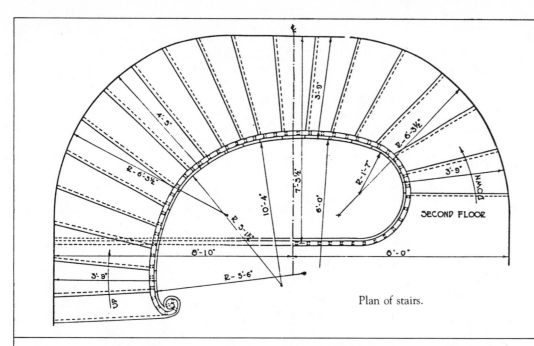

Plan of stairs.

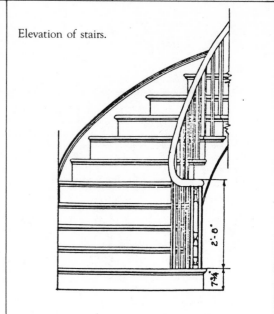

Elevation of stairs.

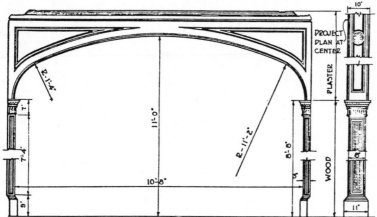

Detail of arch between reception and stair halls.

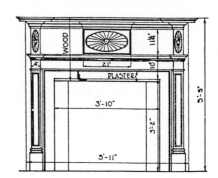

Detail of parlor mantel.

18. Render House

Render House is a somewhat smaller version of Mount Nebo, the house previously illustrated. Rather than a two-story pillared pavilion there is a one-story center section. This house is essentially one story throughout, the attic floor not being of adequate proportions for more than storage.

This house was built c. 1833 in La Grange, Georgia, for Joseph D. McFarland. The architect is thought to have been Collin Rodgers. The original house is the front block of four rooms with a center hall. The rear ell and a side room and porch were added in the late 1800s. The window sash are twentieth century, but were originally 6 lights over 6 lights.

The front entrance is very handsomely composed of paneled double doors, a fanlight, and sidelights. This doorway is identically matched at the rear of the front hall. The Ionic fluted capitals of the porch are of wood with hand-carved capitals.

Two chimneys are located on each side of the older front section; here, both rooms are fitted with a fireplace. There are also two chimneys in the rear section which provide flues for a cooking stove in the kitchen, a dining room fireplace, and back-to-back fireplaces in the bedroom and sitting room. Note the addition of dressing rooms and bathrooms in both sections of the house.

North (front) elevation.

East elevation.

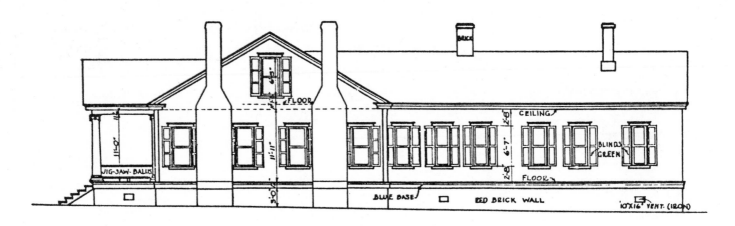

West elevation.

South (rear) elevation

Labels visible in elevation: CEILING, WEATHERBOARD, WHITE, FLOOR, BRICK, BRICK, OPEN, OPEN, BRICK, 4'-0", 2'-8", 3'-0", 4'-6"

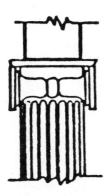

Side view of column capital.

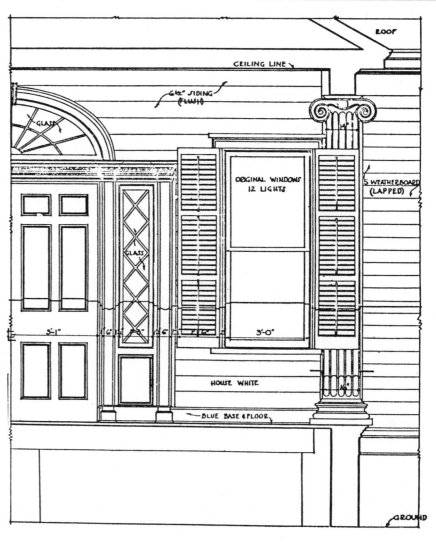

Detail of main entrance.

Labels visible: ROOF, CEILING LINE, 6½" SIDING (FLUSH), GLASS, ORIGINAL WINDOWS 12 LIGHTS, S WEATHERBOARD (LAPPED), GLASS, 3'-0", 5'-1", HOUSE WHITE, BLUE BASE & FLOOR, GROUND

First-floor plan.

Sectional view.

Detail of wainscoting.

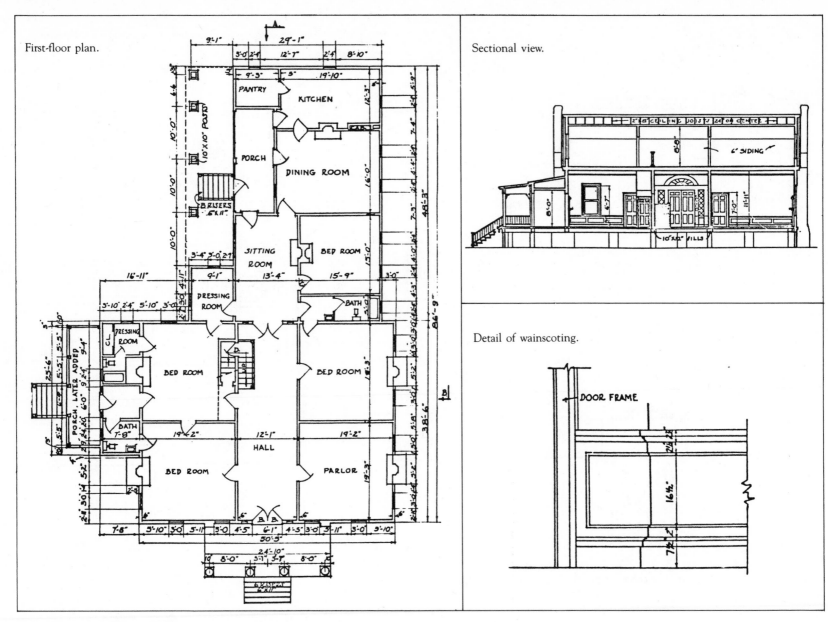

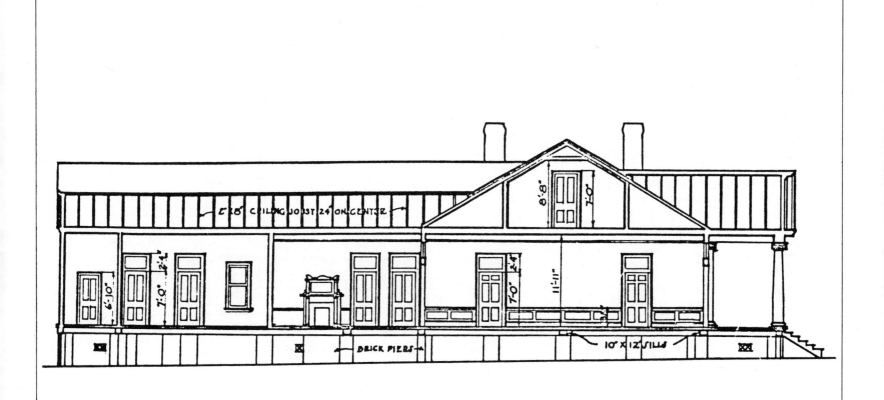

Sectional view.

19. Gaines-Hardy-Roberts House

This stone house, built c. 1835 near Newburgh, Indiana, is representative of a type found in early settlements along the Ohio River. Federal in style, the building follows the classic center-hall plan with four rooms on each floor. Rather than one chimney on each gable end, however, there are two. These are bridged with stone at each end so that the gables are squared off at the peak.

The stonework of the front facade is cut; that of the other walls is random. The precision and balance of the architectural elements—inside and out—lends the house a formal elegance. The front and rear windows parallel each other exactly; so, too, do the front and rear entrances.

Fireplaces are located in each of the eight principal rooms; the largest—for cooking—is naturally in the kitchen. There is a full basement; this floor is partially above ground, and outside light is supplied by narrow windows.

There are a number of handsome features in this practical and tasteful dwelling. The graceful entranceway with double doors, stone trim, and fanlight is striking. Above it is a wrought-iron balcony. Inside, the window sashes are set within simple wood casings which extend to the floor. Extending from the bottom of each window to the baseboard is raised wood paneling. Each window is also fitted with interior shutters.

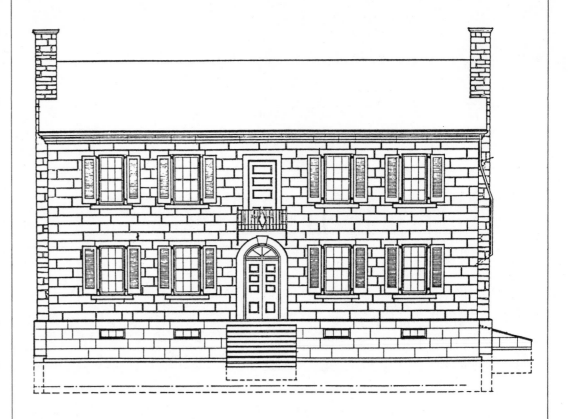

South (front) entrance.

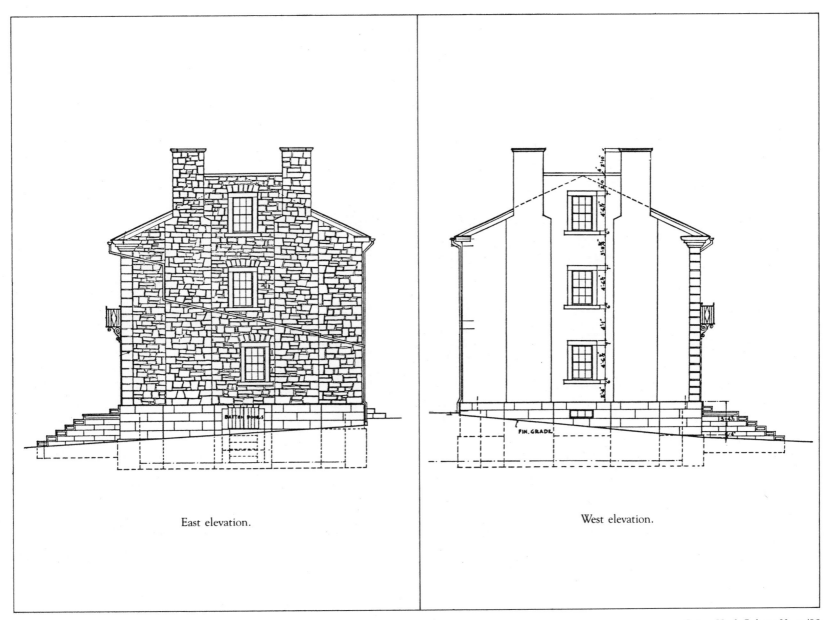

East elevation.

West elevation.

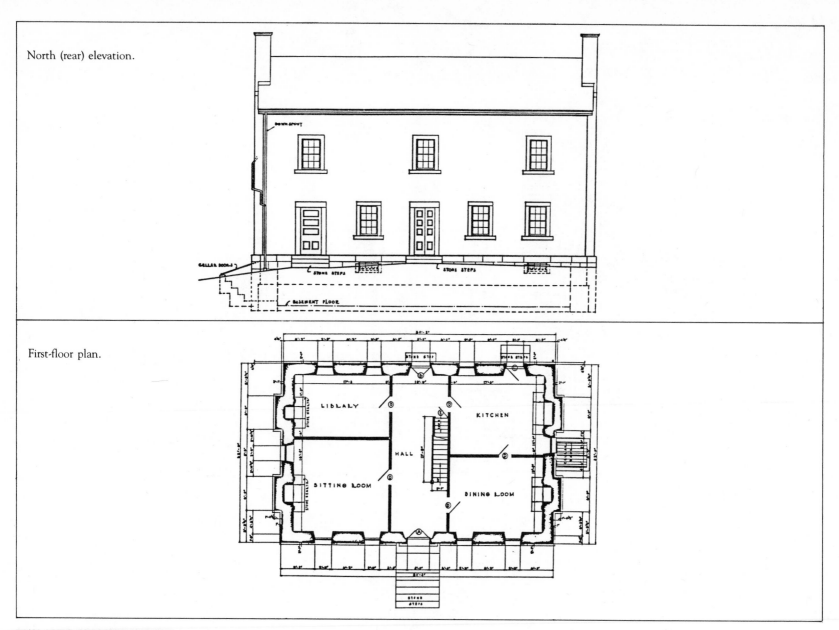

North (rear) elevation.

First-floor plan.

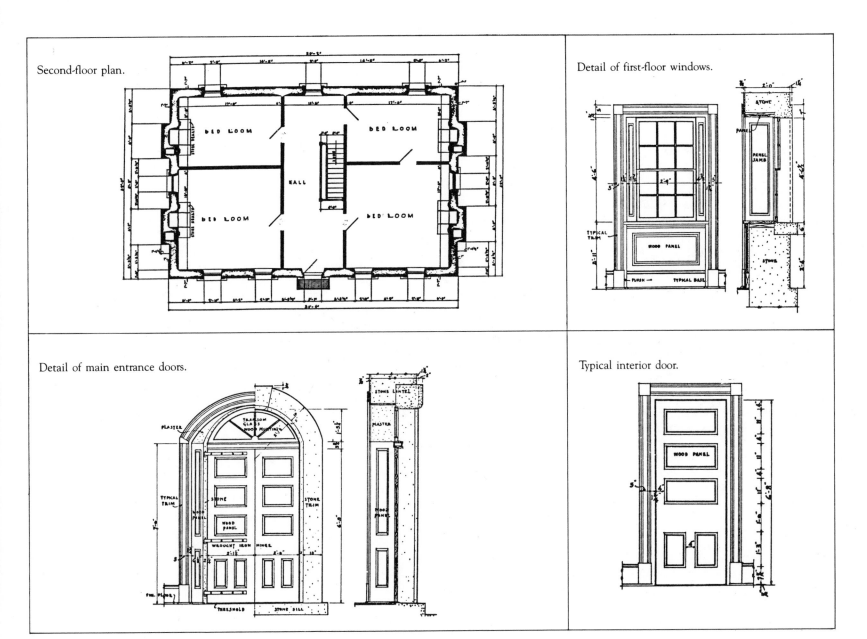

Second-floor plan.

Detail of first-floor windows.

Detail of main entrance doors.

Typical interior door.

20. Mitchell-Roundtree House

This handsome stone dwelling, built in 1837 in Grant County, Wisconsin, appears to be a cottage. In plan, however, the Mitchell-Roundtree House has much in common with larger houses of the Colonial and Federal periods. Here one finds a floor-through center hall on the first floor and an upper center stair hall. The placement of various elements is symmetrical, such as the parallel front and rear entrances and front and rear windows.

A dining room ell projects from the back of the one-room-deep house. A flagstone walk, originally covered, leads from the dining room to a separate kitchen building.

Maximum use is made of the second-story space. Pedimented dormers open up the roof line and provide light on the warm south side of the house. The gable-end chimneys enclose the sides of both first and second floors.

The house is constructed throughout of limestone blocks which vary in thickness between a foot-and-a-half and two feet. Consequently the windows and doors are set in deep reveals. The interior woodwork consists of simple moldings and raised panels. A chair rail is used in all the rooms.

South (front) elevation.

North (rear) elevation.

Typical window elevation (exterior).

Blind

Typical window elevation (interior).

East elevation.

Transverse section.

West elevation.

Typical door elevation.

Wide boards.

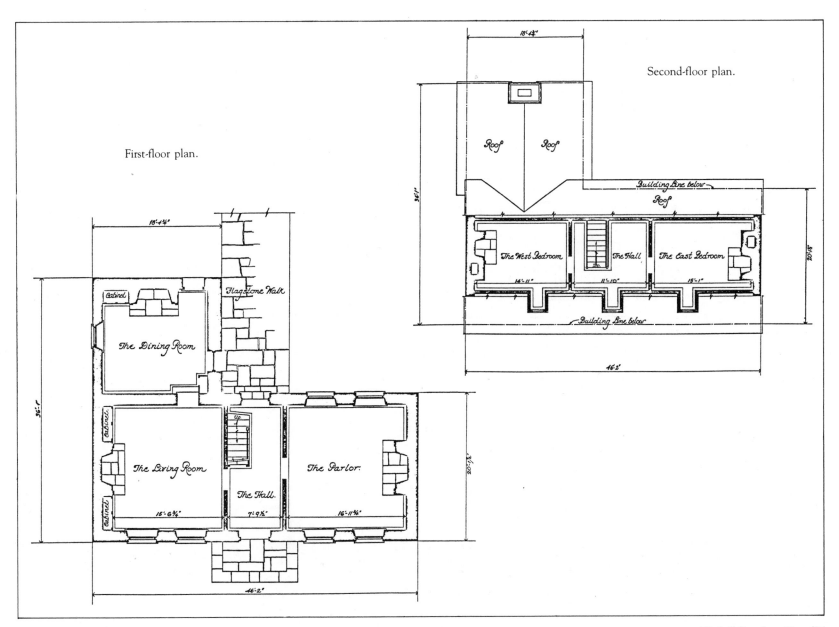

Second-floor plan.

First-floor plan.

Flagstone Walk

Cabinet

The Dining Room

15'-4¾"

36'-1"

Cabinet

The Living Room

15'-6¾"

Cabinet

The Hall

Up

7'-9½"

The Parlor.

16'-11¾"

20'-1¾"

46'-2"

Roof   Roof

36'-1"

Building line below

Roof

18'-4½"

The West Bedroom

14'-11"

The Hall

Dn

11'-10"

The East Bedroom

15'-1"

Building line below

Building line below

20'-1¾"

46'-2"

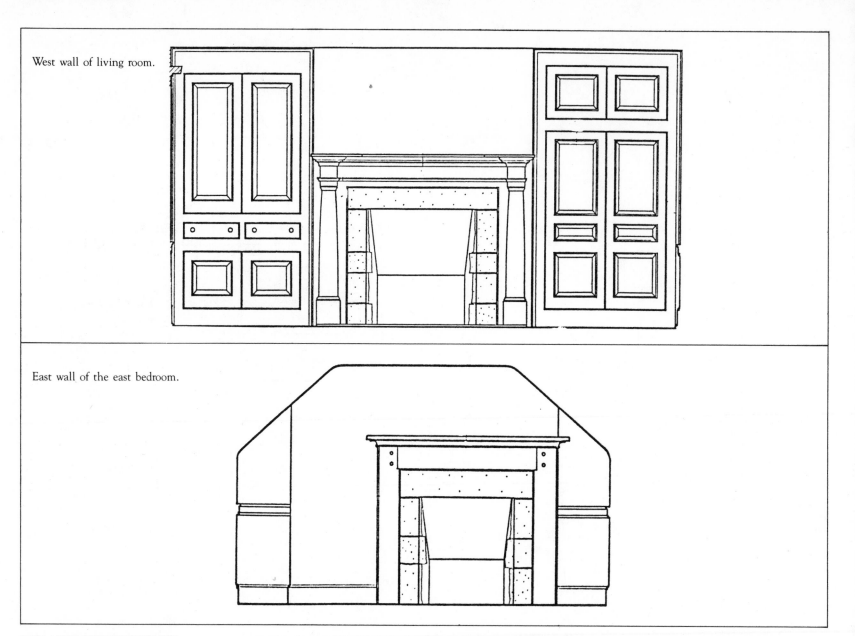

West wall of living room.

East wall of the east bedroom.

21. William T. Bonniwell House

The Bonniwell House near Thiensville, Wisconsin, is a somewhat more formal version of the Mitchell-Roundtree House, previously illustrated. Built in the late 1830s, it is markedly Federal in style. Like the previous house, this house is of fieldstone, but the material has been cemented over and scored to imitate cut stone. The building consists of two full stories rather than one-and-a-half.

In other exterior and interior details, the Bonniwell House is very sophisticated. Especially stylish is the main entrance with fanlight and sidelights, unfortunately now missing its head; the elaborate exterior wood window casings; and the interior window treatments with raised paneling below and at each side.

The floor plan is utterly simple with a center hall on each floor from which the principal rooms open up. Originally, there was a rear wing containing the kitchen, a pantry, and an entry hall, but it has been demolished. The placement of this wing is shown on the first-floor plan and the north elevation. There is a cellar floor under the main surviving section.

Although there are chimneys on each gable end, fireplaces are shown only on one side of the house—in the living room and large bedroom above it. Either there were once fireplaces in the rooms on the opposite side and these have been closed up or these rooms were heated with stoves.

South (front) elevation.

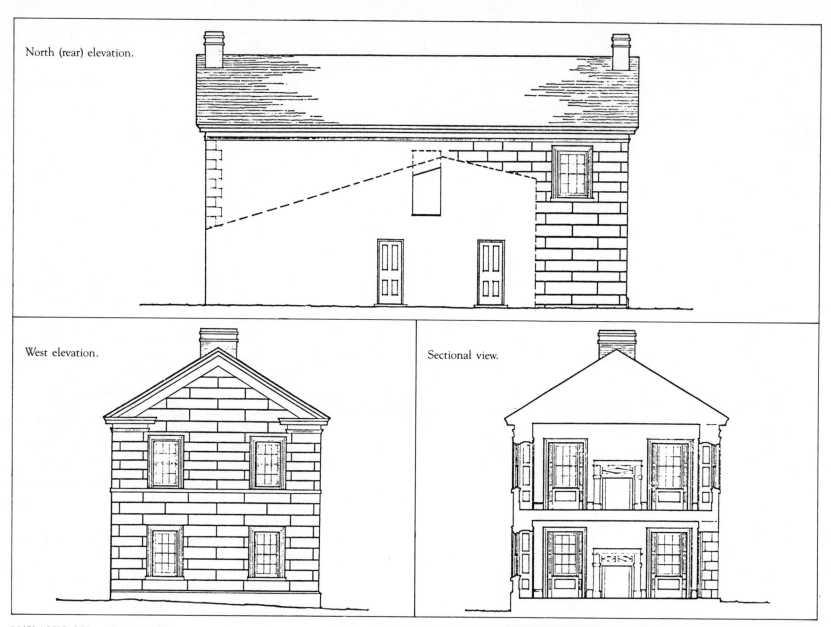

North (rear) elevation.

West elevation.

Sectional view.

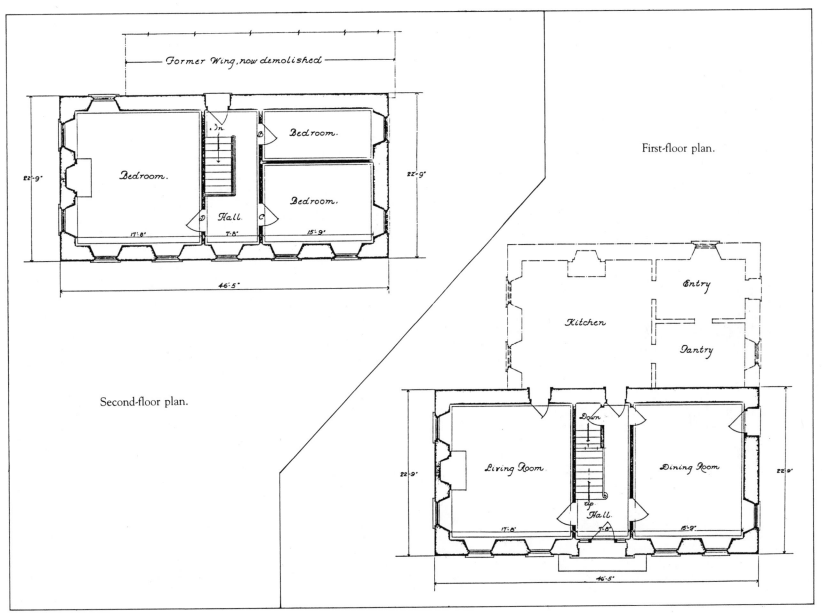

Former Wing, now demolished

Bedroom.

Bedroom.

Dn

Hall.

Bedroom.

22'-9"

22'-9"

17'-8"

7'-8"

15'-9"

46'-5"

First-floor plan.

Second-floor plan.

Entry

Kitchen

Pantry

Living Room

Down

Dining Room

Up.

Hall.

22'-9"

22'-9"

17'-8"

7'-8"

15'-9"

46'-5"

William T. Bonniwell House/99

Interior and exterior window elevations.

Interior and exterior main entrance elevations.

22. Gray House

With columns in antis, a pillared entrance, and frieze windows, the brick Gray House is unmistakably Greek Revival in style. Built between 1836 and 1846 near Connersville, Indiana, it retains, nevertheless, the basic layout of a center-hall Colonial dwelling. The house is two rooms deep with a rear kitchen ell. Two bedrooms are tucked under the low pitched roof. Two other bedrooms are situated on the first floor.

The columns, which project slightly, but not completely, from the front facade, proceed in the same fashion around the sides of the building. Only the brick wall of the rear is unbroken except for windows and the kitchen extension. The frieze windows, set in an unusually wide entablature, also continue around the sides. The entablature wraps around each corner of the rear wall.

Fireplaces are found only in the two front rooms—the parlors on each side of the entry hall. The presence of additional stacks or flue pipes indicates that the remaining rooms were at one time heated by stoves. The garage attached to the kitchen is a later addition. The porch on the south side of the ell was enclosed at one time and is a particularly ungainly and inappropriate "improvement."

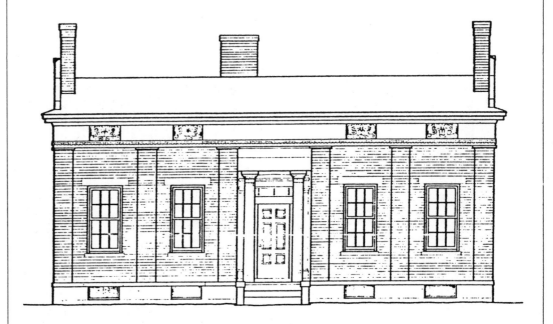

West (front) elevation.

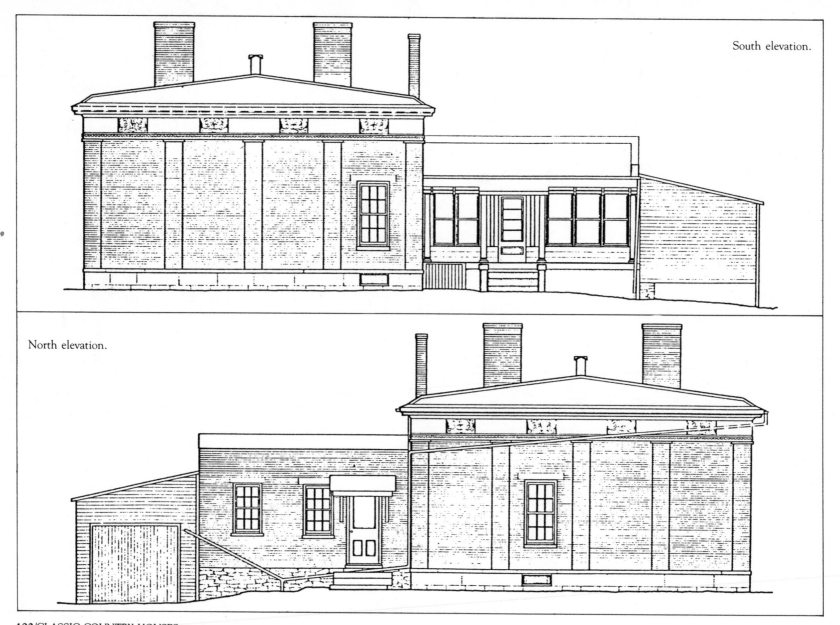

South elevation.

North elevation.

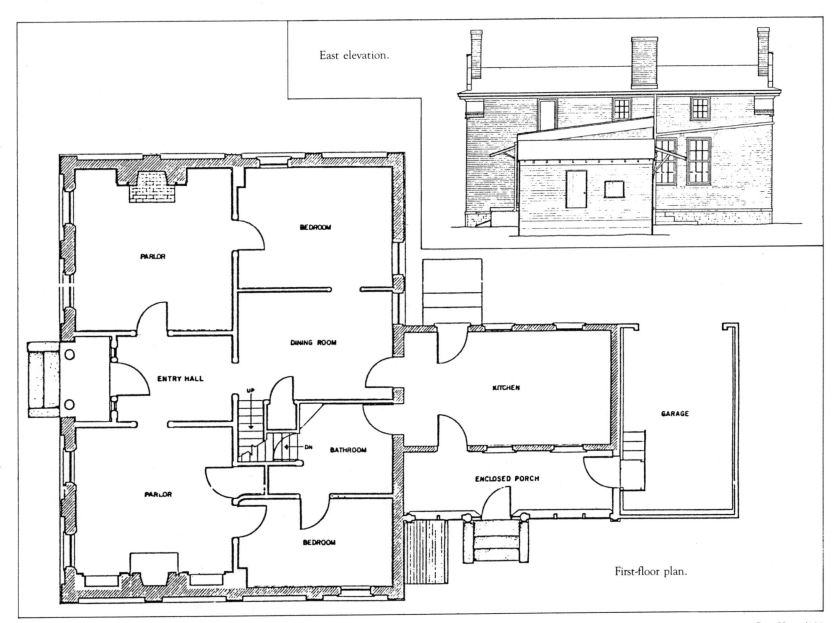

East elevation.

PARLOR

BEDROOM

DINING ROOM

ENTRY HALL

UP

DN

BATHROOM

PARLOR

BEDROOM

KITCHEN

GARAGE

ENCLOSED PORCH

First-floor plan.

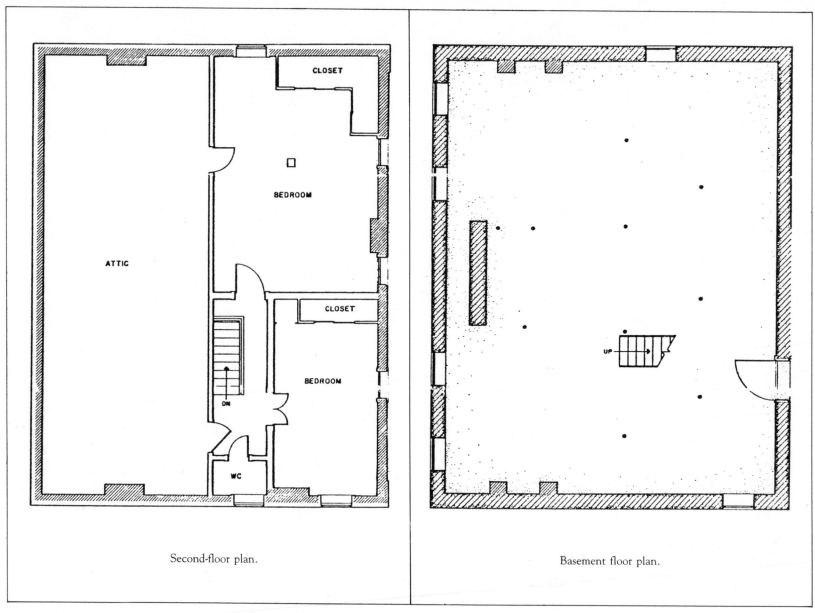

Second-floor plan.

Basement floor plan.

23. Stevenson House

The Stevenson House is a quite typical example of a common nineteenth-century farmhouse. It cannot be described precisely as Federal, Colonial, Georgian Colonial, or Greek Revival. Many architectural historians would term the building "vernacular." It is a hybrid—as most American houses are—a building that combines a Federal doorway with a Greek Revival paneled frieze and cornice. At each gable end there is a lunette in the center of the tympanum of the pediment roof.

The house was built in two portions in rural Erie County, Pennsylvania. The one-story rear section came first in 1824; the two-story main house was added in 1844. The center-hall floor plan of the front section is traditional. The space is intelligently divided into a large living room with a small bedroom and storeroom behind and, on the other side of the hall, a dining room with a pantry and large closet behind. From either the center hall or the pantry, one can enter the rear section of the house with its kitchen, summer kitchen, second pantry, and storeroom.

The only fireplace is found in what is called the summer kitchen, a room that probably served as the only kitchen until the 1840s. There are flues serving other rooms, stoves for heating having become common for cooking and heating by mid-century.

The second floor is divided like the first into three rooms on each side, one of which is a walk-in closet. The rear rooms, however, open up only to the rooms in front of them and not to the center hall, an inconvenient arrangement, but one that could be easily corrected.

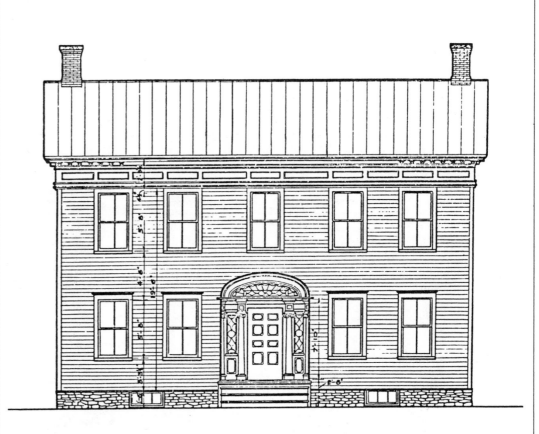

South (front) elevation.

West elevation.

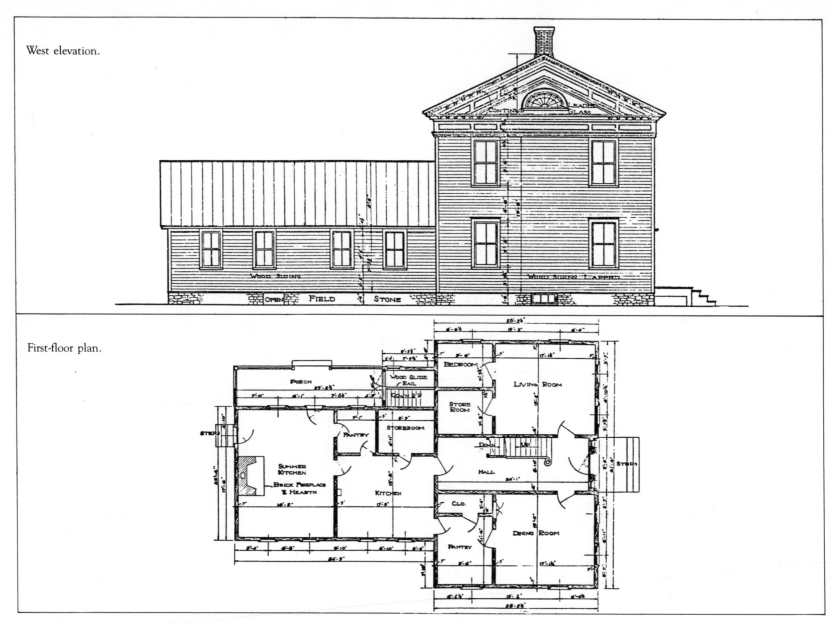

First-floor plan.

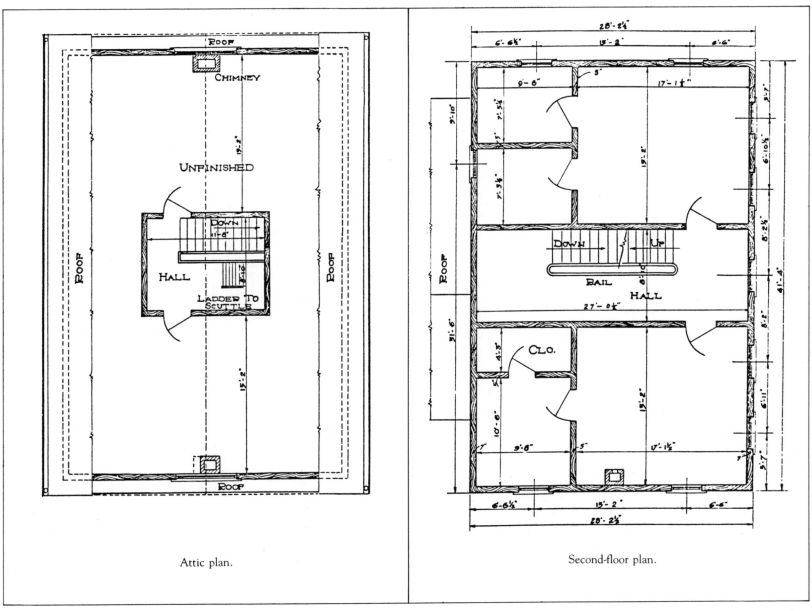

Attic plan.

Second-floor plan.

Interior and exterior elevation of front entrance.

24. Brick House, Willow Dale Farm

It is difficult to date this farmhouse precisely, but it appears to have been built in the 1830s or '40s. Located near Paxtang in Dauphin County, Pennsylvania, the building is very much like many other rural houses of the mid-nineteenth century. Its plan is that of a center-hall Colonial, and chimneys are located at each gable end. The front porch and decorative wood window heads are later additions.

The rear portion of the building has fieldstone walls and is connected to the main section by a frame passageway. The stone section probably served originally as a summer kitchen; the room marked "D" on the first-floor plan was the regular kitchen. The present use of these rooms is unknown.

Five bedrooms open onto a second-floor center hall. Only one of these rooms is fitted with a fireplace; the room opposite it, however, could have been supplied with a stove as there is a chimney flue on this side of the house. The attic floor has two windows at each gable end; the space is not partitioned for bedrooms. There is one separate area which appears to have been a storage room for trunks and other family possessions.

South (front) elevation.

West elevation.

East elevation.

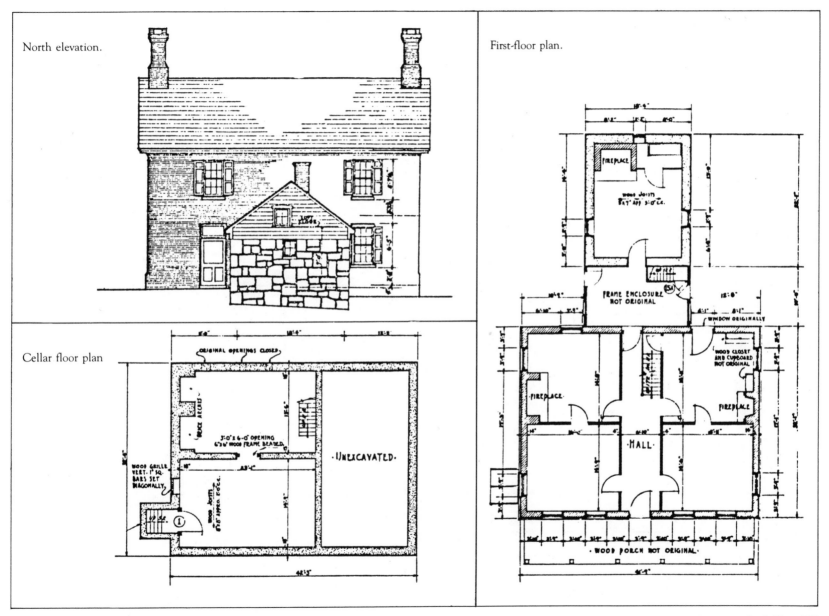

North elevation.

First-floor plan.

Cellar floor plan

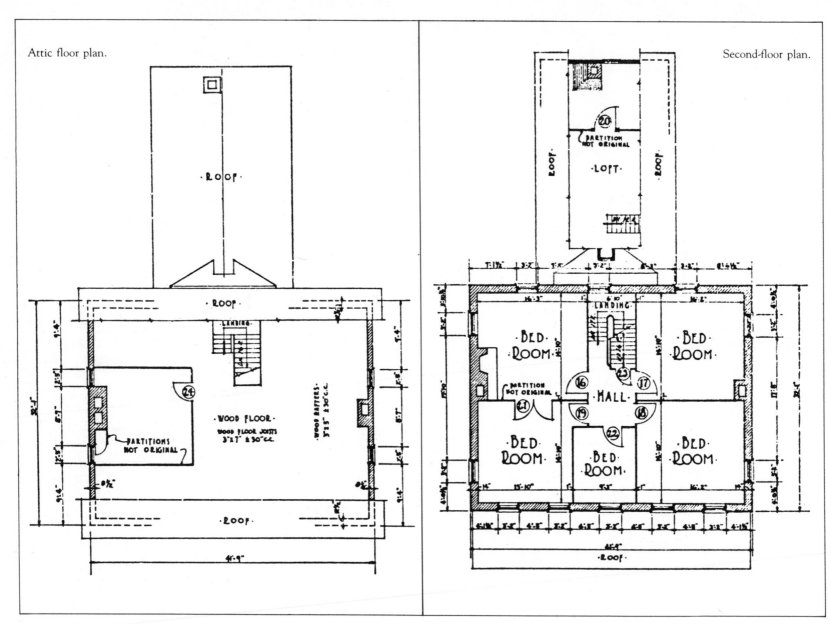

Attic floor plan.

Second-floor plan.

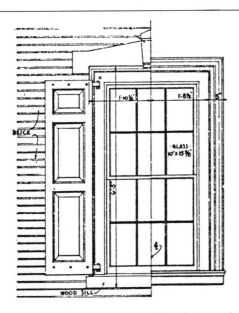

Exterior and interior elevation of first-floor window.

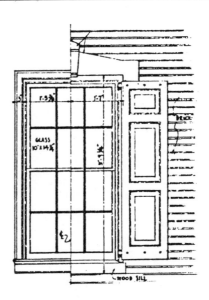

Exterior and interior elevation of second-floor window.

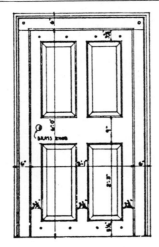

Elevation of exterior door to summer kitchen.

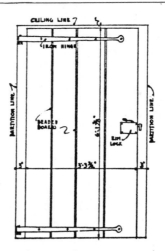

Elevation of interior door in summer kitchen.

25. Booth House

A compact and stylish dwelling, the Booth House was built near Saylesville in Waukesha County, Wisconsin, in 1852. The front of the house is constructed of 10-inch coursed ashlar; the other walls are of random ashlar. The lintels and sills are of wood. The main entrance is typical of those found on Greek Revival houses of the period and features sidelights, side panels, and a raised panel door.

The Booth House has an unusual roof line and gable eaves which flare out at the front and the back of the building. A broad cornice drops below the eaves to form a decorative band across the front and back.

Although Greek Revival in style, the house has an ordinary center-hall floor plan. It appears that the kitchen originally occupied one side of the main section. Sometime later a new kitchen was built as a rear frame addition. On the second floor four bedrooms lead off a center hall. There is a fifth small room for storage at the front end of the hall.

The interior woodwork is simple but sophisticated. Window casings are made up of a series of moldings that extend to the floor. Interior shutters are fitted at each side of the sash, and below the sash is a paneled dado.

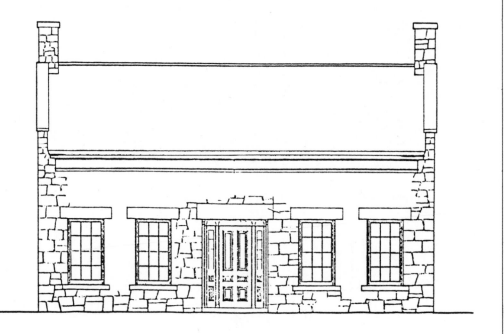

North (front) elevation.

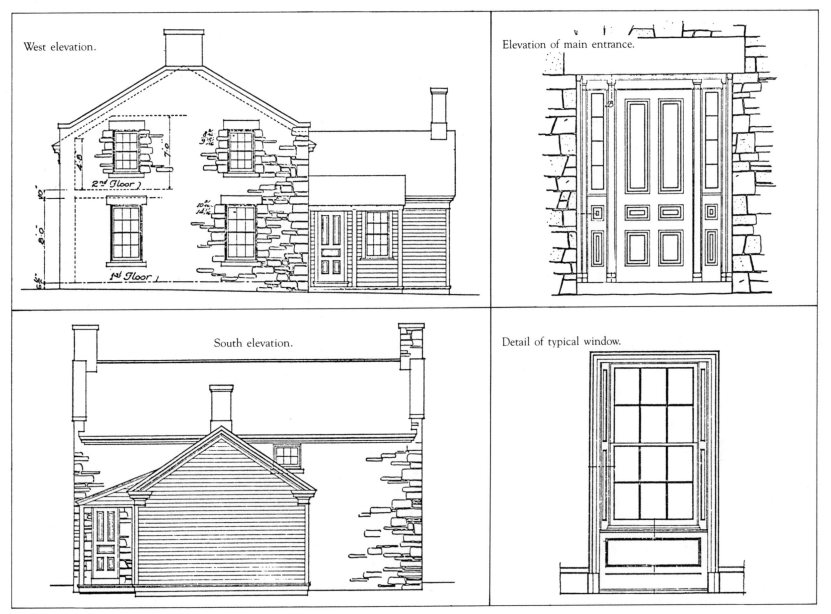

West elevation.

2nd Floor

1st Floor

Elevation of main entrance.

South elevation.

Detail of typical window.

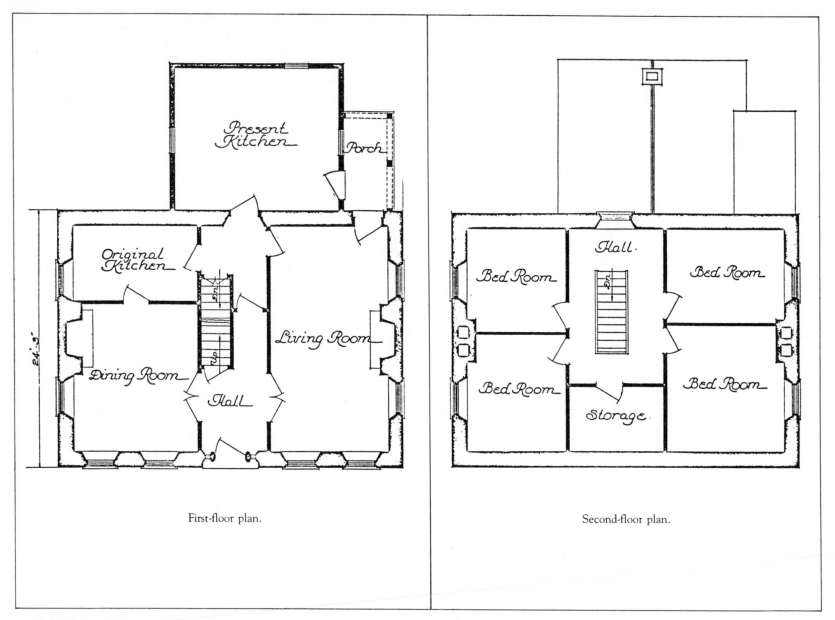

Present Kitchen

Porch

Original Kitchen

Living Room

Dining Room

Hall

24'-3"

First-floor plan.

Hall.

Bed Room

Bed Room

Bed Room

Bed Room

Storage

Second-floor plan.

26. Charles Miller House

Like the Booth House, this dwelling is located in rural Waukesha County, Wisconsin. The Miller House is slightly larger and was built six years later, in 1858. The floor plan is similar, however, and one wonders whether the same builder might have constructed both houses.

There are three rooms in the first-floor front portion, four rooms above them, and a rear ell. The first-floor walls of the rear extension are of stone and appear to have been built at the same time as the front section. The frame porches and second story of this wing appear to be later additions.

Improvements were made to the house in the late 1800s or early 1900s. There are two baths on the second floor, one in the front section of the house and the other *en suite* with the large rear bedroom.

Lintels, sills, and cornice are of wood. On the north or front facade, the stonework is of coursed limestone. Rubble stone is used on the side and rear facade. All of the walls have been plastered, a common waterproofing technique of the time.

The only fireplace is located in the library. A chimney near each gable end, however, would have provided proper ventilation for a stove.

North (front) elevation.

East elevation.

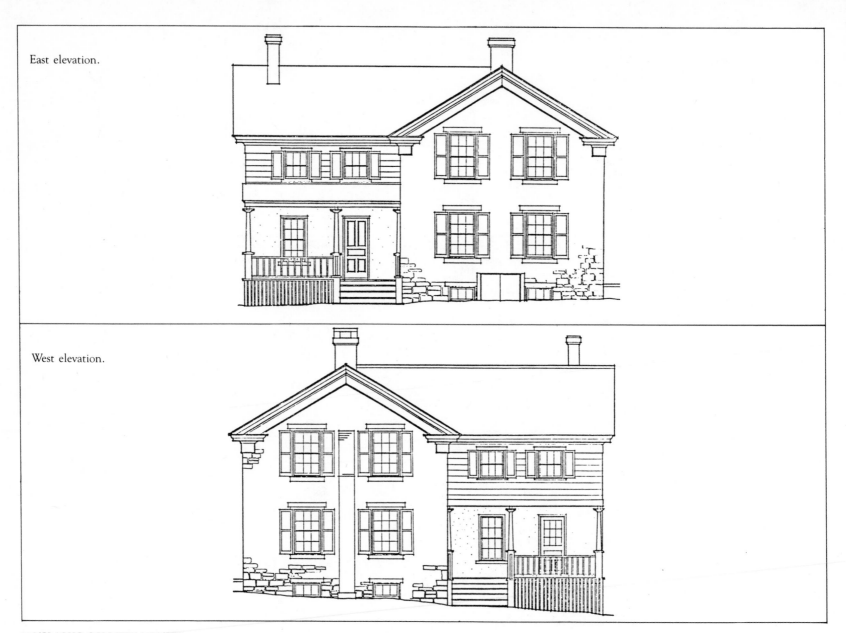

West elevation.

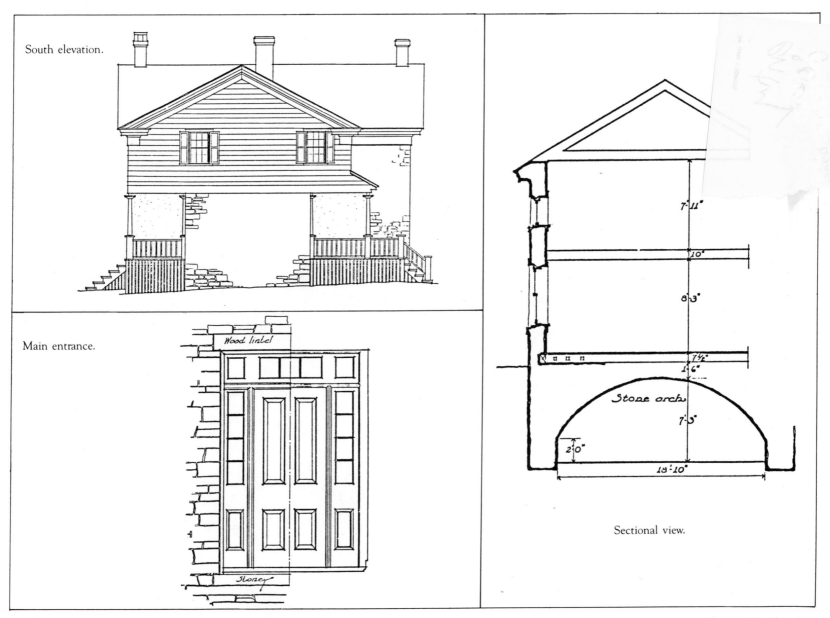

South elevation.

Main entrance.

Wood lintel

Stone

Sectional view.

7'·11"

10"

8'·3"

7½"

1'·6"

Stone arch

7'·3"

2'·0"

13'·10"

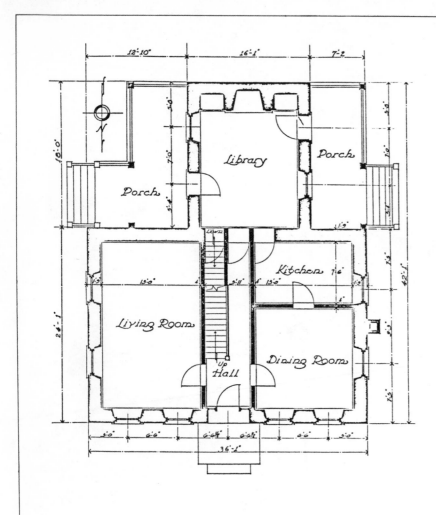

First-floor plan.

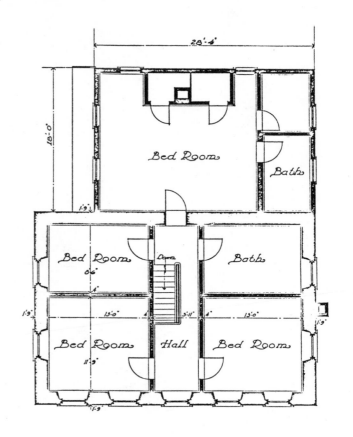

Second-floor plan.

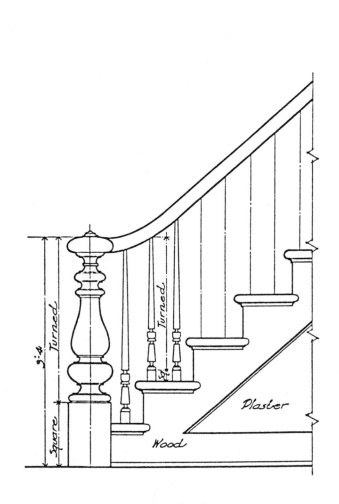

Library detail.

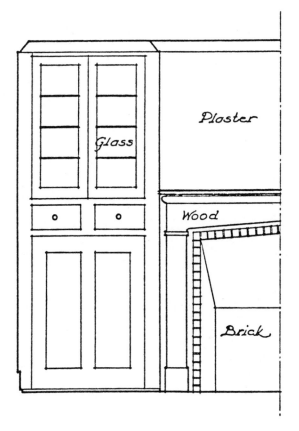

Stair detail.

Selected Bibliography

BERG, DONALD J. *Country Patterns: A Sampler of American Country Home & Landscape Designs from Original 19th-Century Sources.* Pittstown, N.J.: The Main Street Press, 1986.

BLUMENSON, JOHN J.-G. *Identifying American Architecture: A Pictorial Guide to Styles and Terms, 1600-1945.* Nashville, Tenn.: American Association for State and Local History, 1977.

CUMMINGS, ABBOTT LOWELL. *The Framed Houses of Massachusetts Bay, 1625-1725.* Cambridge Mass.: Harvard University Press, 1979.

DOWNING, ANDREW JACKSON. *The Architecture of Country Houses.* Reprint of the 1850 ed. New York: Dover Publications, 1969.

_____. *Cottage Residences.* Reprinted as *Victorian Cottage Residences,* 1873 ed. New York: Dover Publications, 1981.

GROW, LAWRENCE. *Classic Old House Plans.* Pittstown, N.J.: The Main Street Press, 1984.

_____. *Country Architecture.* Pittstown, N.J.: The Main Street Press, 1985.

_____. *More Classic Old House Plans.* Pittstown, N.J.: The Main Street Press, 1986.

_____. *The Old House Book of Cottages and Bungalows.* Pittstown, N.J.: The Main Street Press, 1987.

GWILT, JOSEPH. *The Encyclopedia of Architecture.* Reprint of the 1867 ed. New York: Bonanza Books, 1982.

LOTH, CALDER AND JULIUS TROUSDALE SADLER, JR. *The Only Proper Style: Gothic Architecture in America.* Boston: New York Graphic Society, 1975.

POPPELIERS, JOHN, S., ALLEN CHAMBERS, JR., AND NANCY B. SCHWARTZ. *What Style Is It? A Guide to American Architecture.* Washington, D.C.: The Preservation Press, 1984.

RIFKIND, CAROLE. *A Field Guide to American Architecture.* New York: New American Library, 1980.

SMITH, G. E. KIDDER. *The Architecture of the United States.* 3 vols. Garden City, N.Y.: Anchor Press/Doubleday, 1981.

VAUX, CALVERT. *Villas and Cottages.* Reprint of the 2nd ed., 1864. New York: Dover Publications, 1970.

WHIFFEN, MARCUS. *American Architecture Since 1780: A Guide to the Styles.* Cambridge, Mass.: The M.I.T. Press, 1969.

Illustration Credits

For information regarding any of the following houses, inquiries should be made in writing to the Division of Prints and Photographs, Library of Congress, Washington, D.C. 20450. Given with the name of the property below is the Historic American Buildings Survey number.

1. Berkeley Plantation, VA-363; 2. Fort Bowman, VA-909; 3. Rocky Mills, VA-146; 4. The Cliffs, PA-185; 5. The Lindens, MA 2-3; 6. Tate House, ME-3-7; 7. Jefferds Tavern, ME-43; 8. Bowman-Carney House, ME-45; 9. Jarathmael Bowers House, MA-2-17; 10. Fort Hunter Mansion, PA-38; 11. Rock Ford, PA-368; 12. Coleman-Hollister House, MA-2-19; 13. Marshall House, KY-20-14; 14. Musterfield House, MA-2-25; 15. Moorhead House, PA-51; 16. Shoemaker House, PA-22; 17. Mount Nebo, GA-14-4; 18. Render House, GA-14-62; 19. Gaines-Hardy-Roberts House, IND-24-13; 20. Mitchell-Roundtree House, WIS-28-4; 21. William T. Bonniwell House, WIS-28-7; 22. Gray House, IND-108; 23. Stevenson House, PA-55; 24. Brick House, Willow Dale Farm, PA-35; 25. Booth House, WIS-132; 26. Charles Miller House, WIS-28-11.